# Inhalt

# Vorwort

Wer sagt eigentlich, dass Englischlernen nicht spannend ist? Mit diesem packenden englischen Krimi kannst du schnell und einfach deine Englischkenntnisse verbessern und vertiefen. Alle schwierigen Vokabeln sind unten auf der Seite übersetzt, sodass du keine Schwierigkeiten haben wirst, den Krimi zu verstehen. Für alle Fälle gibt es zu jedem Kapitel eine kurze Inhaltsangabe auf Deutsch.

Nach jedem Kapitel kannst du verschiedene Grammatik- und Wortschatzübungen lösen. Alle Übungen beziehen sich auf fünf wichtige Themen des Englisch-Lehrplans für deine Klasse. Am Ende des Buches findest du eine Grammatikübersicht und ein Vokabelverzeichnis.

Have fun!

# Cat detectives

"**Turn** it **down** kids, it's late," Pete Wilson's dad called into the garage.

Pete had just finished a furious guitar solo. He rolled his eyes.

"Dad, how are we supposed to become the world's greatest rock band without practice?"

"I thought you were detectives, not rock stars," his father replied with a **grin**.

Pete turned to his two best friends – Anna, a pretty twelve-year-old on bass guitar, and Raymond, also twelve, on drums.

"That's all for tonight, I guess."

"Oh, by the way, have you seen the paper?" Mister Wilson held up the local newspaper. "It's a story about three young detectives solving the case of Miss Warner's missing cat."



**to turn down**: leise stellen
**grin**: Grinsen

"Wow," Pete took the newspaper, "a photo of us on the front page!"

"You guys look **cute** in that picture," Anna **teased**. "Cuter than the cat."

"Tall, dark and **handsome**?" Raymond asked **with a twinkle**.

"Congratulations, Detectives," Mister Wilson smiled, "but tomorrow is the first day of school. Time to go home."



The next day, Pete, Raymond and Anna walked into their new classroom. Boomer, the **bully**, **mocked**, "I say, Sherlock, have you found my cat?" The class **burst out laughing.** Embarrassed, the kids sat down as their teacher entered.

"Welcome to Greenville Junior High School. My name is Miss Barnes." Blond,

**cute**: niedlich
**to tease**: hänseln
**handsome**: gut aussehend
**with a twinkle**: augenzwinkernd
**bully**: brutaler Kerl, Schulhoftyrann
**to mock**: verspotten
**to burst out laughing**: in Gelächter ausbrechen

**petite** Miss Barnes looked around the classroom.

"Some of you seem familiar," she nodded toward Pete, Anna and Raymond.

"Those are the detectives," Boomer Morgan called out. The class again **erupted** in laughter.

"The cat detectives from the newspaper," Miss Barnes smiled, "how very cute!"

Pete and his two friends **blushed**.

"I'd like to introduce a couple of students new to the area." Miss Barnes announced. "Benson Aquiline?"

A **timid** "Yes" was heard from a pale, **stout** boy. He looked nervously around the room and smiled shyly.

"Welcome Benson," Miss Barnes said gently. "Please tell the class a little about yourself."

**petite**: zierlich
**to erupt**: ausbrechen
**to blush**: erröten
**timid**: schüchtern
**stout**: korpulent

"Well," the boy's voice **trembled**, "I moved here from San Diego. My dad is the new president of Greenville Bank."

He sat down again.

"Luke Jones is another new face. Luke?"

A **skinny** kid with shoulder-length hair stood up and **bowed** to the class, which brought on laughter. He wore **torn** jeans and his T-shirt advertised a hard rock band. Luke Jones did not appear to be shy at all.



"I moved here from Bakersfield, live in the **trailer park** and my dad hasn't found a job yet. As a matter of fact, he's still on the couch watching TV."

Luke sat down **amid** amused **chuckles**.

Miss Barnes shook her head with a sad little smile. "Luke, welcome to Greenville.

**to tremble**: zittern
**skinny**: dünn
**to bow**: sich verbeugen
**torn**: zerrissen
**trailer park (am.) / caravan site (brit.)**: Wohnwagensiedlung
**amid**: inmitten
**chuckle**: Kichern

Hopefully your dad will find a job soon."

Three hours later the kids ate lunch in the crowded school cafeteria.

"What a day," Anna **sighed,** as she bit into a peanut butter toast. "I hope Junior High gets better than this."

Before Pete could answer, Anna pointed to where Boomer and friends were approaching the table.

"Here comes trouble," she whispered.

"Well, if it isn't the pet detectives." Boomer took Raymond's soda and emptied it in one gulp. He **crushed** the **can** and **tossed** it on the table.

"Hey," Raymond protested. "Stop that!"

The bully **seized** Raymond by the shirt collar and pulled the boy close.

"One more word out of you and I'll **beat you to a pulp**."

**to sigh**: seufzen
**to crush**: zerdrücken
**can**: Dose
**to toss**: werfen
**to seize**: greifen
**to beat sb. to a pulp (ugs.)**: jdn. zu Brei schlagen

"Leave him alone!" Pete demanded.

Boomer turned to Pete.

"What are you going to do about it?"

Pete stood up. "My friends and I stick together."

Anna stood up as well. "That's right."

"You **wimps** against us?" Boomer Morgan tore Anna's sandwich from her hand and stuck it on Pete's shirt front. The sandwich left a large peanut butter **stain.**



"Now what are you going to do?"

Pete looked down at the peanut butter on his shirt. The whole cafeteria was silently watching.

"You kids break it up!" Vice Principal Smith ran toward the group. Boomer and his friends walked off.

"That was close," Pete sighed and sat down.

"Today might have been the worst day

**wimp (ugs.)**: Schwächling
**stain**: Fleck

of my life," Anna **muttered** as Pete and Raymond walked home on either side of her. "How humiliating."

Pete **shrugged**. "Let's try to avoid Boomer and find a real case to work on."

Raymond shook his head. "I think we should concentrate on the band. That will get us more respect than being cat detectives."

"Cat detectives," Pete **murmured** and flushed again.



Anna and Pete had been neighbors and close friends since pre-school. A **tomboy**, she grew up playing baseball and climbing trees. Ever since Pete's dad had given the family garage to his son, she spent most of her time there. Raymond joined the two shortly after he moved to town. He had worked odd jobs and saved up enough

**to mutter**: murmeln
**to shrug**: mit den Achseln zucken
**to murmur**: murmeln
**tomboy**: Wildfang

money to buy a drum set. It was his most **prized** possession.

Pete's father was a detective at the Greenville Police Department. Shortly after Pete was born, his mother had left the family. Mister Wilson had to raise his son by himself. **According** to his few friends, he had done an excellent job.

"Okay, I'll be right over," Pete's dad said into the phone as Pete walked into the kitchen the next morning.



"What's up so early, dad?"

Mister Wilson hugged his son. "Someone broke into your school last night and left a mess. Up to now we have not had to worry about vandals in Greenville."

"What did they do?"

"Graffiti was sprayed. Scary stuff, according to the school **janitor**. Have you heard any rumors about gangs, son?"

**prized**: wertvoll
**according**: gemäß, nach, laut
**janitor (am.) / custodian (brit.)**: Hausmeister

"Not a thing. This is not Los Angeles, dad."

"True," Mister Wilson said. "Well, time to go."

"Alright, dad. See you."

The longer Pete thought about the news, the more he began to worry. Gangs in Greenville? For the first time in many years, Pete felt a faint fear.



## Short cut

*Pete, Anna und Raymond finden Mrs. Warners entlaufene Katze, doch die entsprechende Zeitungsmeldung verursacht am ersten Schultag nur Heiterkeit bei den Klassenkameraden. Die Katzendetektive nehmen sich vor, endlich einen richtigen Fall zu übernehmen – der sich mit der über Nacht graffitibesprühten Schule zu bieten scheint.*

## Übung 1

*Welches der folgenden Wörter passt in welche Lücke?*

broken / was / solved / introduced / spent

1. Pete, Anna and Raymond had ______________ the case of Miss Warner's missing cat.
2. The three kids ______________ most of their time in Pete's garage, playing music in a band.
3. Pete's father ______________ a detective.
4. At school after the summer holidays, their teacher ______________ two new students to the class: Benson and Luke.
5. The next morning, Pete's father told him that someone had ______________ into their school the night before and sprayed graffiti.

## Übung 2

*Buchstabensalat! Um welche Wörter handelt es sich?*

1. v-e-t-i-t-d-e-c-e-s: ______________
2. r-e-t-a-h-e-c: ______________
3. l-b-y-l-u: ______________

## Übung 3

*Suche in diesem Rätsel das Simple Past (Einfache Vergangenheit) der folgenden unregelmäßigen Verben:*

| | | | |
|---|---|---|---|
| hold – | ______________ | stand – | ______________ |
| take – | ______________ | eat – | ______________ |
| sit – | ______________ | can – | ______________ |
| say – | ______________ | leave – | ______________ |

| | | | | | | | |
|---|---|---|---|---|---|---|---|
| H | E | L | D | Z | U | K | A |
| E | D | E | S | T | G | I | W |
| C | I | T | T | A | R | S | E |
| A | Y | S | T | O | O | D | N |
| M | A | L | C | L | P | Z | T |
| E | Q | D | E | A | T | I | A |
| C | O | U | L | D | Z | G | T |
| S | X | B | Y | I | T | L | E |
| E | K | N | E | S | K | E | D |
| A | Q | U | D | V | A | F | U |
| I | W | F | L | I | F | T | P |
| A | Y | K | A | L | E | O | H |
| S | D | A | F | E | Q | O | J |
| A | F | X | L | F | H | K | I |
| I | A | D | E | T | K | A | S |
| D | S | A | I | D | E | D | K |

## Übung 4

*Welche Wörter passen hier? Die Buchstaben in den umrandeten Kästchen ergeben in der richtigen Reihenfolge einen Namen.*

1. The kids would like to become the world's greatest _ □ _ _ _ _ _ _.

2. They practiced regularly in Pete's _ _ □ _ _ □ .



3. Anna played the □ _ _ _ _ _ _ _ _ _ _.

4. Pete played the guitar and Raymond the _ _ _ □ _.

5. At _ _ _ □ _ _, the three kids had trouble with their classmate Boomer.

Lösungswort: □ □ □ □ □ □

## Übung 5

*Aus zwei mach eins! Verbinde die beiden Sätze mithilfe des Relativpronomens* ***who****.*

Anna was a tomboy. The tomboy grew up playing baseball and climbing trees.

Anna was a tomboy **who** grew up playing baseball and climbing trees.

1. Pete's father was a detective. The detective had done a great job raising his son.

   Pete's father was a detective ____________________

   ____________________________________________

   ____________________________________________

2. Benson was a shy boy. The shy boy moved there from San Diego.

   Benson was ____________________________________

   ____________________________________________

   ____________________________________________

3. Luke was a skinny kid. The skinny kid wore torn jeans and a T-shirt.

   Luke was ______________________________________

   ____________________________________________

   ____________________________________________

# Break-in

“Did you hear what happened?” Pete and Raymond nodded as Anna jogged toward them.

“It was on the morning news,” Raymond replied, “and Pete’s dad is already **investigating**.”



Several police cars were parked in front of the school, and students stood in the parking lot. Two policemen guarded the entrance to the building.

“Kids,” the cop warned, “you can’t go in there.”

“But my dad is Detective Wilson,” Pete explained.

“I don’t care, get over there with the other kids. Now!”

“They don’t need pet detectives, huh?” Boomer **yelled**. His two **buddies** laughed

**to investigate**: ermitteln
**to yell**: schreien, brüllen
**buddy (am.) / chum (brit.)**: Kumpel

dutifully.

"Shut up, Boomer," Raymond replied.

Anger turned the bully's face bright red. "Want a bloody nose?"

Just then, Mister Wilson stepped through the door.

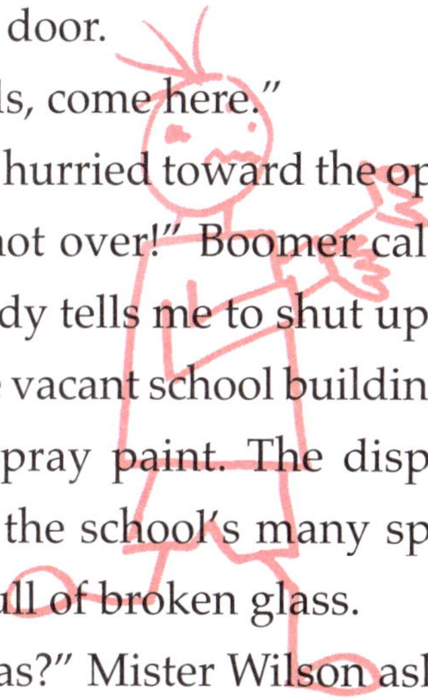

"Pete, kids, come here."

The three hurried toward the open door.

"This is not over!" Boomer called after him. "Nobody tells me to shut up!"

Inside the vacant school building, the air **reeked** of spray paint. The display case which held the school's many sports trophies was full of broken glass.

"Any ideas?" Mister Wilson asked.

The kids looked around. There was purple spray paint everywhere: on the walls, windows, **lockers** and doors to the classrooms.

The three youngsters shook their heads.

"Mister Wilson, why would anyone do

**to reek**: stinken, riechen
**locker**: Schließfach

this?" Raymond asked.

"Hard to say," Detective Wilson nodded. "Why would anyone **vandalize** someone else's property?"

Pete pointed at a large symbol painted on the wall. "Looks like something out of a hip-hop video."

"That's why I thought you kids might be able to help us. If anyone knows MTV, it's you three. But," Mister Wilson shook a warning finger, "keep in mind, that this is a crime. I don't want you kids to get in the way of the police."



"But, we can help investigate, right?"

"No investigating. What I need from you is to keep your eyes and ears open."

As darkness fell, the kids sat in Pete's garage.

"No investigating," Pete **grumbled,** "even my dad thinks of us as pet detec-

**to vandalize**: zerstören
**to grumble**: murren

tives." Anna **strummed** her bass guitar while Raymond played a slow beat on the drums.

"Maybe we really should give up the detective business," Anna said.

"No way!" Pete responded loudly. "My dad doesn't have to know everything we do. We can prove how good we are!"

The trio **launched into** a very loud version of an endless Led Zeppelin song. Afterward, Anna **unplugged** her bass guitar and turned to her grinning friends. "That sounded great. We're getting there."

"From outside, I thought Led Zep was in the garage," Mister Wilson said as he walked through the door.

Pete leaned his guitar against the wall. "Dad, what's happening in the graffiti case?"

"Well, nothing new, except that it points



**to strum**: klimpern
**to launch into**: in Gang bringen, einleiten
**to unplug**: den Stecker herausziehen

to what **currently** goes on in big cities."

"Gangs, Mister Wilson?" Raymond asked.

"Gangs. One of the symbols we found spray-painted at the school looks like one used by a Southern California gang. It's a bad sign." Mister Wilson **glanced** at his **wristwatch**. "Time to pack up, kids."

As his dad left the garage, Pete turned to his friends. "So there could be gangs in Greenville? Man, this is getting good."



"Son, wake up." Pete's alarm clock by the bed read 1:30 am.

"I just got a call. The grocery store on Main Street was broken into." As Detective Wilson stood up, Pete noticed the gun under his jacket. "Go back to sleep. I didn't want to leave without telling you."

"Dad," Pete sat up, "be careful."

Mister Wilson nodded and left the room.

**currently**: zur Zeit
**to glance**: einen Blick werfen
**wristwatch**: Armbanduhr

When Pete heard his father's car pull out of the driveway, he **bolted out** of bed and called Anna's cell phone.

The girl carefully opened her window and climbed out into the **backyard**. She **tip-toed** to the garden gate.

"Hey."

The whisper **startled** Anna.

"It's me, Pete." The boy stood up.

Anna **slapped** his shoulder. "You scared me."



"I told Raymond to meet us in Main Street Park."

Detective Wilson parked next to Morton's Grocery Outlet. The store's side door had been **forced** open.

"Officer Callahan," Wilson called to one of the officers on the scene, "what's the status?"

**to bolt out**: hinausstürzen
**backyard**: Garten (am.), Hinterhof (brit.)
**to tiptoe**: schleichen
**to startle**: aufschrecken
**to slap**: einen Klaps geben
**to force**: aufbrechen

The **wiry** policeman shook his head. "Broken bottles, shelves overturned, and the same type of graffiti we had at the school."

Pete, Anna and Raymond stood behind tall bushes in the park across from the grocery store. The red and blue **emergency lights** of the police cars illuminated the dark building.

Somewhere, a twig **snapped**.



"Quiet, someone is coming!" Pete whispered. A shadowy figure took cover behind a tree and watched the grocery store. The three friends **dared** hardly breathe. Then Raymond, who was **kneeling**, lost his balance and fell into the bush in front of him. The shadow behind the tree looked up and quickly ran along the park's edge. For an instant, the kids were able to make

**wiry**: drahtig
**emergency lights**: Blaulicht
**to snap**: knacken
**to dare**: wagen
**to kneel**: knien

out a face in the flashing police lights.

"Wow", Pete whispered, "that was Luke, the new kid!"

## Short cut

*Die Verwüstung der Junior High gibt der Polizei Rätsel auf. Petes Vater bittet die drei Detektive, die Augen offen zu halten. Dann wiederholt sich die Zerstörung; doch dieses Mal beobachten die drei, wie Luke vom Tatort flieht.*

## Übung 6

*Setze die folgenden Sätze ins Passiv.*

Someone broke into the grocery store.

The grocery store was broken into.

1. Someone forced the store's side door open.

___

___

2. Someone broke a lot of bottles.

___

___

3. Someone sprayed graffiti on the walls.

___

___

## Übung 7

*Wie könnte man den folgenden Satz ins Passiv setzen, ohne Informationen zu verlieren?*

The emergency lights of the police car illuminated the dark building.

___

___

## Übung 8

*Kreuzworträtsel! Wie heißen diese Wörter auf Englisch?*

1. antworten
2. erklären
3. bewachen
4. ermitteln
5. warnen
6. bemerken

*Tipp: Alle diese Verben kommen im zweiten Kapitel vor!*

## Übung 9

*Vervollständige die folgenden Sätze im Past Perfect (Vorvergangenheit).*

1. The night before, someone ________________ ____________ (break) into the school building.
2. He ________________________ (spray) graffiti everywhere.
3. He __________ also ______________________ (vandalize) the display case that held the school's sports trophies.
4. The three kids wondered why he __________ ______________ (do) that.



## Übung 10

*Rätsel! Welches englische Wort wird hier erklärt?*

This is an aggressive kid who likes to frighten his classmates.

Lösung: ________________________________

## Übung 11

*1, 2 oder 3? Welches der drei Wörter passt? Die dazugehörigen Zahlen ergeben in der Summe 9.*

1. The three kids wanted to help Pete's father, but he told them, "No ☐ !"
   (1) vandalizing
   (2) investigating
   (3) bullying
2. He just asked them to ☐ their eyes and ears open.
   (1) keep
   (2) close
   (3) nod
3. In the park across from the grocery store, the kids ☐ someone running away.
   (1) looked
   (2) listened
   (3) saw
4. It was Luke, their new ☐ .
   (1) friend
   (2) detective
   (3) classmate

Summe: ☐

# Benson

After only a few hours sleep, Pete woke to the sound of the alarm clock. "Why was Luke hiding in the park?" he thought to himself as he brushed his teeth. His dad had come home just after Pete. Now he was **snoring** loudly on the couch downstairs. Pete quietly left the house.

Anna and Raymond met Pete at the end of the street. Both looked very tired. "I could have slept another couple of hours," Anna **yawned**.



"Let's keep an eye on Luke today." Raymond suggested.

Anna nodded. "Let's also try not to **get beaten up** by Boomer and his friends."

The kids stopped at the crosswalk. Across the street, a luxurious Lincoln towncar had pulled up to the **curb**. The passen-

**to snore**: schnarchen
**to yawn**: gähnen
**to get beaten up**: verprügelt werden
**curb (am.) / kerb (brit.)**: Bordstein

ger door opened, and a **chubby** boy climbed out. The large man driving said something to the boy, who kept walking away.

"Look, it's Benson," Anna remarked as the kids crossed the street. They soon caught up with Benson, who was still trying to ignore the fat man in the town-car.

"Benson, since it is the chauffeur's day off, someone from the bank will be picking you up. Do not be late!"

"Okay, dad, I'm not a little kid anymore, leave me alone!" Benson called.

Surprise showed on his face as Pete, Anna and Raymond caught up with him.

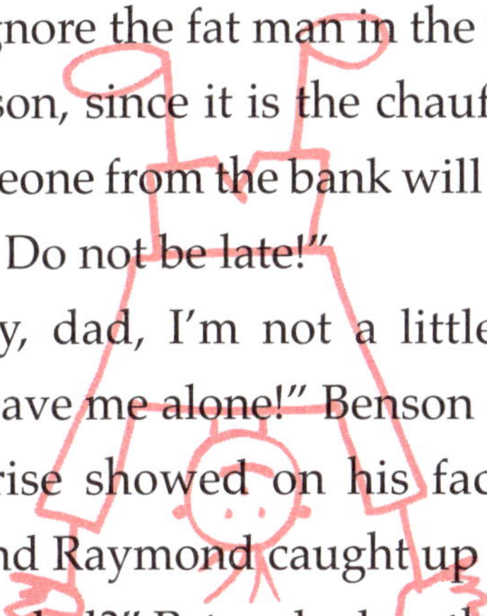

"Your dad?" Pete asked, as the town-car drove off.

"Yes, my **overprotective** dad. Too often, he treats me like a baby," Benson muttered.

"I'm Pete, and these are my best friends Anna and Raymond."

**chubby**: rundlich
**overprotective**: überbesorgt

Benson nodded. "Nice to meet you. Say, you're the detectives from the newspaper article."

"Yeah, go ahead and laugh, I don't care anymore," Raymond grumbled.

"Why would I laugh? I think it's cool."

"Really?" Pete was **pleased**. "So far, we don't have many fans."

Pete was trying hard to stay awake as Miss Barnes **droned on** about American history. Anna, who sat next to him in class, tried to get his attention.



"Look," she whispered.

Pete looked up. Luke was drawing something onto his notebook, which was covered with names of popular rock bands. Pete struggled to **decipher** some of the drawings, but Luke sat too far away.

"I have an idea," Anna whispered. She reached into the backpack by her feet.

**pleased**: zufrieden
**to drone on**: eintönig reden
**to decipher**: entziffern

"Anna!" Miss Barnes approached the girl. "Let's see if you were paying attention: Where is the Bay of Pigs?"

Surprised, Anna sat up. There was absolute silence in the classroom.

"Cuba?" she answered with a smile.

"Very good!" Miss Barnes **exclaimed** and continued on with her lecture.

"Good thing you are as clever as you are," Pete whispered.

Anna smiled and drew a digital camera from her backpack as Miss Barnes wrote on the blackboard. She hid the **device** behind her book and pointed it toward Luke.

As the bell rang, Miss Barnes ended her lecture. "Don't forget, the **homework assignment** is due tomorrow."

The kids met outside the classroom.

"Did you get some pictures?" Pete wanted to know.

**to exclaim**: ausrufen
**device**: Gerät
**homework assignment**: Hausarbeit, Schularbeit

Anna nodded. "High resolution."

"What does that mean?" Raymond asked.

"Lots of pixels. The higher the more detail without losing sharpness."

Pete and Raymond were **impressed**. Anna was not only smart, she was a great photographer as well.

"Hi, **do you mind** if I join you for lunch?" Benson had caught up to the group.



Pete looked at his friends, and then turned to the new kid. "Not at all. Come on, let's go to the cafeteria."

The group sat around a table, eating and **chatting**. Benson spoke about his move from San Diego to Greenville, how he had loved the big city and how he missed his friends. The conversation stopped when Luke walked past them. The three detec-

**impressed**: beeindruckt
**do you mind**: stört es dich (euch)
**to chat**: plaudern

tives watched closely as the boy sat down at a table.

"Something wrong, kids?" Benson inquired. "You are all **staring at** Luke. He sure likes to keep to himself, doesn't he?"

"So, Benson, do you play an instrument?" Raymond asked, attempting to change the subject.

Benson nodded. "Classical piano. I've been taking lessons for years. I **favor** keyboards though."



"**No kidding**?" Pete turned to Benson. "We formed a band a while ago. Rock stuff. Raymond on drums, Anna on bass, and I play the guitar."

"We could use a keyboard player," Anna said.

"If you are interestec bring your keyboards to my garage ton.ght, six o'clock," Pete offered. "Let's see what you can do."

**to stare at sb.**: jdn. anstarren
**to favor (am.) / favour (brit.)**: bevorzugen
**no kidding (ugs.)**: im Ernst

“Hey, Wilson!” The kids turned around. It was Boomer and his group of **goons**.

“Tell your dad to leave my brother alone,” Boomer hissed.

“Your brother? What are you talking about?”

“I’d look out if I were you,” Boomer walked off.

“Who is he?” Benson whispered.

“Just some guy who won’t leave us alone.”



“My sister knew Boomer’s brother Jake until he **dropped out** of high school,” Raymond explained to the kids. “From what she said, he was always stealing stuff and vandalizing other kids’ property. He’s much worse than Boomer.”

“I’ll ask my dad what is going on,” Pete decided.

At home Pete talked to his dad.

“Boomer Morgan said that you are after

**goon (ugs.)**: Schläger
**to drop out**: abbrechen

his brother. What's the story?"

"Jake Morgan was **picked up** just around the corner from the grocery store, sitting in his car with a back seat full of stolen goods."

"Is he a **suspect** in the graffiti case?" Pete wondered.

"You know I can't tell you details. But believe me, if someone with his criminal background is caught near a crime scene, he has to be the main suspect."



## Short cut

*Luke macht sich verdächtig, Benson spielt gut Keyboard, und die Kids sind überrascht, als Petes Vater bekannt gibt, dass Boomers großer Bruder ein alter Kunde der Greenviller Polizei ist und im Graffitifall der Hauptverdächtige.*

**to pick up**: aufgreifen
**suspect**: Verdächtiger

## Übung 12

*Vervollständige die folgenden Sätze im Past Continuous (Verlaufsform der Vergangenheit).*

Pete wondered why Luke ________________ (hide) in the park.

Pete wondered why Luke **was hiding** in the park.

1. Pete's father __________________________ (snore) loudly on the couch downstairs.

2. Benson __________________________ (try) to ignore the fat man in the car.

3. Luke __________________________ (draw) something onto his notebook.

4. The teacher said, "Let's see if you __________ __________________________ (pay) attention."

5. Boomer's brother _________________ always _________________ (steal) things and _________________ (vandalize) other kids' property.

## Übung 13

*Suche in diesem Rätsel das Simple Past (Einfache Vergangenheit) der folgenden unregelmäßigen Verben:*

wake – ____________ draw – ____________

think – ____________ hide – ____________

keep – ____________ ring – ____________

catch – ____________ meet – ____________

*Tipp: Du findest alle diese Vergangenheitsformen im dritten Kapitel!*



| | | | | | | | |
|---|---|---|---|---|---|---|---|
| H | I | D | D | Z | U | K | T |
| E | D | E | S | T | G | I | H |
| C | I | T | T | A | R | S | O |
| F | Y | S | K | O | O | D | U |
| W | O | K | E | L | P | Z | G |
| E | Q | D | P | A | R | I | H |
| C | O | U | T | D | A | G | T |
| S | X | B | Y | I | N | L | E |
| E | K | N | E | S | G | E | D |
| A | Q | C | D | V | A | F | U |
| M | W | F | A | I | F | T | P |
| A | E | K | A | U | E | O | H |
| S | D | T | F | E | G | O | J |
| A | F | X | L | F | H | H | I |
| I | A | D | E | T | K | A | T |
| D | R | E | W | D | E | D | K |

## Übung 14

*Welches der folgenden Wörter passt in welche Lücke?*

great / digital / decipher / impressed / smart

1. In class, Pete tried to ____________________ what Luke was drawing, but the boy sat too far away.
2. Anna drew a ____________________ camera out of her backpack and took photos of Luke's drawings.
3. Pete and Raymond were ____________________.
4. Anna was a ____________________ girl and a ____________________ photographer.



## Übung 15

*Buchstabensalat! Um welches Wort handelt es sich hier?*

w-e-h-m-o-o-r-k s-g-a-i-e-m-t-s-n-n:

________________________________________

*Tipp: Der Begriff hat etwas mit Schule zu tun!*

## Übung 16

*Vervollständige die Bedingungssätze. Achte dabei auf die richtige Zeitform: Simple Present im if-Satz, will-Future im Hauptsatz.*

Pete said, "If you ________________ (want), I ________________ (ask) my dad what is going on."

Pete said, "If you **want**, I **will ask** my dad what is going on."

1. Boomer hissed, "If your dad ________________ ________________ (not leave) my brother in peace, you ________________________ (be) in trouble."

2. Raymond said to Benson, "If you ____________ ________________ (play) the keyboard, we ________________ (be) happy to have you in our band."

3. Pete said, "If we ________________________ (not stop) investigating, my dad ____________ ____________ (be) angry."

# Luke

The sounds of The Doors' "L.A. Woman" echoed through Pete's garage. All eyes were on Benson, who had just finished an **incredible** keyboard solo. Anna stepped to the microphone and sang the final verses of the song.

"Wow!" Pete yelled after the song was over. "You sure know how to play the keyboards!"



"Shall we play another **tune**?" Anna asked the group.

"No, not right now," Pete replied. "It's time for detective business."

He told his friends about the conversation with his father and what he had found out about Boomer's brother.

"But what about Luke? What was he doing in the park that night?" Anna asked.

"What are you talking about?" Benson

**incredible**: unglaublich
**tune**: Melodie

looked surprised.

"Can you keep a **secret**?" Pete asked his new friend. Benson nodded.

"Yes, Luke definitely sounds like a suspect," Benson said after listening to Pete's story.

"Anna, show him the photos you took of Luke's drawings in class," Raymond **suggested**.



The girl nodded and pulled a laptop computer from her bag. The computer screen showed one of the photos of Luke drawing on his notebook.

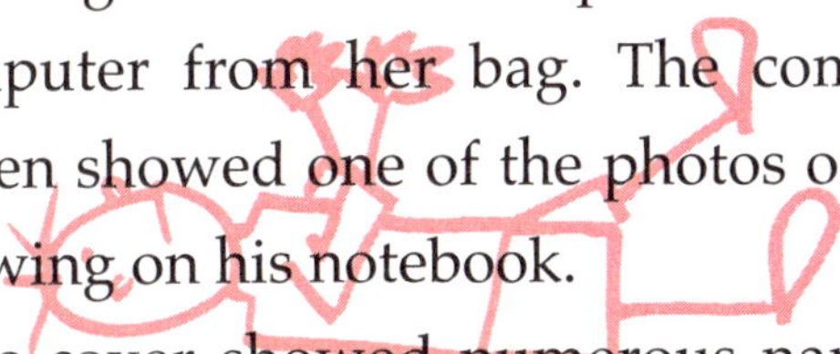

Its cover showed numerous names of rock bands, among well-drawn **skulls and crossbones**.

"He is quite a good artist," Benson said. "Which does not make him a graffiti bandit, of course."

**secret**: Geheimnis
**to suggest**: vorschlagen
**skulls and crossbones**: Totenköpfe und gekreuzte Knochen

"You're right," Anna replied, "but the fact that he was at the scene of the crime and his **stealthy** behavior there make him a suspect. Tomorrow after school, let's follow him!"

"Pete, there he is!" Anna **grabbed** Pete's arm. The two had been waiting near the main entrance of the school since the final bell rang. Raymond and Benson would meet them later while Pete and Anna followed Luke.



The thin boy **strolled** down Madison Avenue, with Pete and Anna cautiously **trailing** him on the shaded side of the street. At one point, Luke stopped and put on a pair of headphones. He continued walking, occasionally playing air-guitar and whistling to the music only he could hear. At Harry's **Hardware Store** on Main

**stealthy**: verstohlen, heimlich
**to grab**: zufassen
**to stroll**: schlendern
**to trail**: verfolgen
**hardware store**: Haushaltswarenladen

Street, Luke looked around without noticing the two kids following him and went inside.

Pete and Anna crossed the street and carefully approached the store window. They could see Luke as he walked toward a display labeled Art and Paint Supplies.

"What the hell are you kids doing? Get out of here!" Red-faced Harry, the hardware store owner, **stomped** toward the two as they stared through the shop window. Startled, they turned to Harry.

"S-sir," Pete **stammered**, "we're just looking through your window."

"Darn kids, always making trouble," Harry grumbled. "Get out of here before I call the cops!"

Pete and Anna hurried to the corner.

"Let's go back across the street so Luke won't see us."



**to stomp**: stapfen
**to stammer**: stottern

Moments later, Luke **exited** the store holding a brown paper bag.

"I'll bet he's got spray paint in that bag," Anna whispered.

Luke took his time going home. He led Pete and Anna on a **winding** tour of Greenville, stopped for an ice cream and sat in the park for almost ten minutes before continuing on to the trailer park.



The boy passed **shabby** trailer homes and broken-down cars. Small children played **unsupervised** among broken bottles and trash, yellow dogs snuffled hungrily at **garbage strewn** around mobile homes. Luke stuffed the paper bag into his backpack and disappeared in one of the trailers.

"Pete," said Anna, "the sun is setting. Let's go home before we get in trouble. It's

**to exit**: verlassen
**winding**: gewunden
**shabby**: schäbig
**unsupervised**: unbeaufsichtigt
**garbage (am.) / rubbish (brit.)**: Abfall, Müll
**to strew**: verstreuen

after seven o'clock."

Pete nodded. "I'm going to call Raymond. Maybe he can take over for us while we check in at home."

Pete called Raymond on his cell phone, gave him **directions** to Luke's trailer, asked him to invite Benson along and **promised** he would wait for him to arrive.

It was after ten o'clock when Pete returned to the trailer park. Raymond sat behind an old car across from Luke's trailer.



"Hey Pete, I've been sitting alone here for more than two hours, what took you so long?"

"I had to wait for my dad to go back to work before I could leave the house," Pete whispered. "Did anything happen?"

"Absolutely nothing, except that I'm freezing out here! Benson said he would meet us here but he never **showed up**."

**directions**: Wegbeschreibung
**to promise**: versprechen
**to show up**: auftauchen, erscheinen

Pete **hissed** a warning as the door to Luke's trailer was thrown open. The boys watched as a tall, thin man **stumbled** out, holding a bottle of **booze**. He seemed very drunk. Behind him was Luke.

"Dad," Luke whispered, "get back in the house."

The man turned toward Luke, and for a moment it looked as if he would fall over. Luke helped his father back into the trailer. Not long thereafter, he stepped out, locked the trailer door carefully and walked past the hiding kids.

"Let's go," Pete whispered.

"Pete, look!" Raymond pointed to the trailer behind them. A large man stood in front of it. He was holding a much smaller person. In the moonlight shining down through the pines, the boys could tell that the man had one hand firmly over the per-



**to hiss:** zischen
**to stumble:** stolpern
**booze (ugs.):** Fusel

son's mouth, the other was wrapped around the neck. The small body struggled to get free.

"Oh my God, it's Anna!" Pete stammered. Both boys ran over toward the man. The heavy stranger struggled with Anna, who **twisted** and kicked. Suddenly the man screamed in pain and released the girl. Anna ran as fast as she could toward Pete and Raymond. Both boys watched in horror as the man pulled a large, **chrome-barreled** handgun from his **waistband** and pointed it at them.



## Short cut

*Luke kauft Farbe und wird von den Detektiven bis zum Wohnwagenpark verfolgt. Sie sind schockiert über die ärmlichen Verhältnisse dort – und werden unvermittelt von einem bewaffneten Mann bedroht.*

**to twist**: sich winden
**chrome-barreled (am.) / barrelled (brit.)**: mit verchromtem Lauf
**waistband**: Hosenbund

## Übung 17

*Vervollständige die folgenden Sätze im Past Perfect (Vorvergangenheit).*

1. Pete told his friends what he ______________ ____________________ (find) out about Boomer's brother.

2. Anna showed Benson the photos that she ____________________________ (take) in class.



3. The kids suspected Luke because he ____________________________ (be) at the scene of the crime.

## Übung 18:

*Rätsel! Welcher englische Begriff wird hier erklärt?*

This is a computer that you can carry with you in a bag.

Lösung: ____________________________________

## Übung 19

*Kreuzworträtsel! Wie heißen die folgenden Wörter auf Englisch?*

1. flüstern
2. vorschlagen
3. antworten
4. stammeln
5. schreien
6. zischen

*Tipp: Du findest alle diese Wörter im vierten Kapitel!*

## Übung 20

***Who** oder **that**? Setze das richtige Relativpronomen ein.*

1. At the trailer park, Pete and Anna saw small children __________ played unsupervised among the trash.

2. There were yellow dogs ___________ snuffled hungrily at the garbage.

3. Pete called Raymond ____________ agreed to come and take over.

4. Raymond pointed at the trailer ____________ stood behind the boys.

5. A heavy stranger struggled with Anna ______________ tried to kick the man.

6. Then Anna ran as fast as she could toward Pete and Raymond _________ were both watching in horror.

## Übung 21

*1, 2 oder 3? Welches der drei Wörter passt am besten? Die dazugehörigen Zahlen ergeben in der Summe 8.*

1. The door of Luke's trailer was ☐ open.

   (1) kept
   (2) thrown
   (3) closed

2. A tall, thin man ☐ out of the trailer.

   (1) stumbled
   (2) jumped
   (3) ran

3. He held a bottle and looked very ☐

   (1) relaxed
   (2) tired
   (3) drunk

4. Then Luke came out and ☐ his father back into the trailer.

   (1) carried
   (2) helped
   (3) put

Summe: ☐

## Danger at the trailer park

"Run!" Anna screamed as she **zipped** past her friends. Both turned and ran.

"If I ever see you **brats** again, I'll kill all of you!" The thunderous voice of the man sent shivers down Pete's spine. The kids did not stop until they reached the forest. The **gloomy** trailer park lay behind them.



"I had to wait until my parents went to bed before I could sneak out. When I got there, I saw Luke leave, so I hid behind a trailer. It smelled really bad there, like ammonia or something. Next thing I knew, someone grabbed me from behind and started **choking** me."

"What did you do to get away?" Pete wanted to know. Although tears rolled down Anna's cheeks, she smiled a **crooked**

**to zip**: flitzen
**brat**: freches Kind
**gloomy**: deprimierend
**to choke**: würgen
**crooked**: schief

smile, sniffled and said, "I bit his arm. Tasted horrible, but it worked."

Both Raymond and Pete put their arms around her.

"You're very brave, Anna," Pete whispered in her ear. "Let's go home, I think we have had enough action for one night."

There was much excitement at school the next day. Everyone was talking about the latest graffiti **incident**. The **vacant** gas station at the end of town had been broken into, and graffiti once again had been sprayed. The three detectives sat in the cafeteria when Benson approached. He had quite a story to tell.

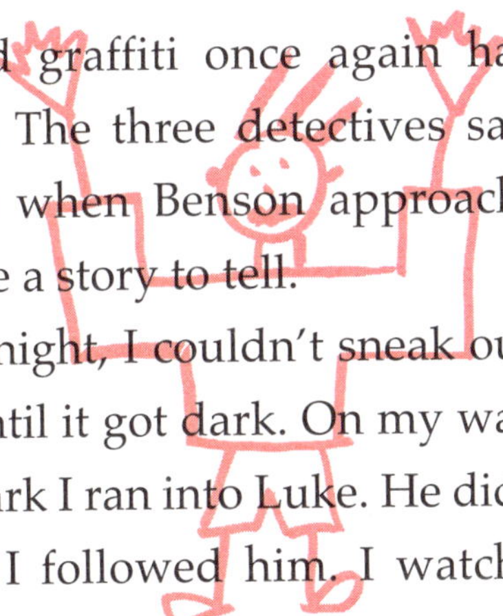

"Last night, I couldn't sneak out of my house until it got dark. On my way to the trailer park I ran into Luke. He did not see me, but I followed him. I watched him break into the gas station. He was plain to see – the moon had just risen, and he wore

**incident**: Vorkommnis
**vacant**: leer stehend

a white T-shirt. Saw him climb through the window and disappear inside!"

"Pete, you have to tell your dad!" Anna said.

Pete shook his head. "I would have to tell him what happened last night, and that would be the end of the case for us."

"Well then, we can't let Luke out of our sight anymore. Not until we have proof he's the **culprit**." Anna seemed **determined**. Over and over, all through the night, she had **relived** the fear she felt. "We must act," she said. "We have to give Pete's dad the means to lock up the criminal."

Anna looked up to see Luke passing by their table. He looked her in the eye, brows **furrowed**, and began to say something. Instead, he shook his head and walked on. She watched him until he passed through the cafeteria door.



**culprit**: Täter
**determined**: entschlossen
**to relive**: wieder erleben
**to furrow**: runzeln

"Think **he's onto us**?" Pete asked. Anna just raised her shoulders. "Who knows?"

The longer the afternoon, the more Pete felt **ill at ease**. There was no **denying** the danger of Anna's situation. He had to let his father know what had happened, but he feared his dad's anger. Pete did not want to risk a **curfew**, which would take him off the street exactly when he was needed most. This was a real case, a **cliffhanger**, a real **page-turner**, and he wanted to be right in the middle of it. The case of the missing cat had shown him the fine line between success and ridicule.



When his father finally came home, Pete sat down with him and gave him a detailed description of all that had happened, about Benson having seen Luke break into

**he's onto us**: er ist uns auf die Schliche gekommen
**ill at ease**: unbehaglich
**to deny**: leugnen
**curfew**: Ausgangsverbot
**cliffhanger**: spannende Sache
**page-turner (ugs.)**: spannendes Buch

the gas station and the man with the gun in the trailer park. Mister Wilson began to get angry, but then reached over and gave Pete a big, fatherly **bear hug**.

"Thank you, Pete, for being honest. You know I could forbid you to leave the house for a month or two – and yet, you had the courage to tell me. Let's go out and get some dinner."

The Hey Let's Eat restaurant was crowded as usual. They ordered a salad, cheeseburger, **fries** and a soft drink.



"Okay, dad," Pete promised, as Mister Wilson asked him to avoid the trailer park. And he agreed to leave his dad a note if he did go out late. In return, Mister Wilson said he would check out the man with the gun and the **bite mark** on his arm. "But I need a reason," he explained. Pete nodded; he knew how difficult a policeman's work

**bear hug**: kräftige Umarmung
**fries (am.) / chips (brit).**: Pommes frites
**bite mark**: Bisswunde

could be. "Which also applies to your friend Benson's **account** of seeing Luke break into the gas station. He may be telling the truth, but it is very hard to prove without evidence such as fingerprints," explained Detective Wilson. Pete knew; he had heard that often enough.

Shortly before lunch, Pete received a call from his dad, who had **to fill in for his boss** at a **trial** in San Geronimo, an hour's drive down the coast. "I will be back tomorrow evening," Mister Wilson said and advised Pete to sleep over at Raymond's house.

After school, Raymond and Pete followed Luke home, leaving him lots of room and occasionally waiting until the boy in front of them finished smoking his cigarette or picked a few berries at the edge of the woods leading to the trailer park.



**account**: Bericht
**to fill in for sb.**: für jdn. einspringen
**trial**: Gerichtsverfahren

"Let's wait here for him to return," Raymond suggested as they passed a parking area a few yards from the trailer park entrance. The boys walked up a **ridge** and **crawled** under a row of bushes at the edge of a clearing, with a perfect view of the trailers, the parking area and the only street leading in and out of the trailer park.



Flies **buzzed** in the afternoon heat, bugs crawled and a dog had a **barking fit**. Pete's eyelids grew heavier, and he **nodded off** in the shade of the bushes. He awoke with a start, only to see a heavy-set man sit down not ten feet from Raymond and himself. His smell was **overpowering**, a mixture of sharp chemical **fumes** and unwashed body. The man carried a cloth bag, and his lower right arm was bandaged. Pete

**ridge**: Grat, felsige Erhöhung
**to crawl**: kriechen
**to buzz**: summen
**barking fit**: Bellanfall
**to nod off (ugs.)**: einnicken
**overpowering**: penetrant
**fumes**: Dämpfe

turned his head to see Raymond's reaction, but Raymond slept with his mouth open, unaware of the danger.

Pete was sure the man was the one who had held Anna captive. What if Raymond made a sound, what if he even turned over in his sleep? They would not be able to get away. And the fat, stinking man was dangerous, probably even more so now that Anna had escaped him. The man with the gun. Pete shivered.



## Short cut

*Annas Abenteuer bewegt Pete dazu, seinem Vater alles zu beichten. Der warnt vor raschem Handeln und verbietet den Detektiven, zum Wohnwagenpark zu gehen. Sie beobachten die Wohnwagen und Luke nun aus sicherer Entfernung. Im Wald treffen sie wieder auf den Mann mit der Pistole.*

## Übung 22

*Vervollständige die Bedingungssätze. Achte dabei wieder auf die richtige Zeitform: Simple Present im if-Satz, will-Future im Hauptsatz.*

1. The man shouted, "If I ____________________ (see) you again, I ____________________ ____________ (kill) all of you!"

2. Pete's father said, "I ____________________ (not be) able to arrest anyone if we ____________________ (have) no evidence such as fingerprints."

3. Pete thought, "If Raymond ____________________ (make) a sound, the man ____________________ (find) us."



## Übung 23

*Buchstabensalat! Um welches Wort handelt es sich hier?*

a-i-f-r-i-t-g-f: ____________________

## Übung 24

*Das Past Participle brauchst du, um das Passiv zu bilden. Finde in diesem Suchrätsel das Past Participle der folgenden Verben:*

see: ____________________

break: ____________________

spray: ____________________

| | | | | | | |
|---|---|---|---|---|---|---|
| O | I | A | T | Z | K | E |
| L | B | R | O | F | W | K |
| H | A | R | L | L | P | G |
| E | I | D | O | A | T | P |
| Z | F | D | N | K | Z | T |
| S | P | R | A | Y | E | D |
| E | K | N | E | E | K | N |
| E | T | U | L | V | N | F |
| N | W | H | D | I | F | D |



## Übung 25

*Vervollständige nun die folgenden Sätze mit diesen Partizipien.*

1. A vacant gas station had been ________________ into.
2. Once again, graffiti had been ________________.
3. Luke had been ____________________ at the gas station.

## ◯ Übung 26

*Vervollständige die folgenden Sätze im Past Continuous (Verlaufsform der Vergangenheit).*

1. At school everyone ______________________ (talk) about the latest graffiti incident.
2. After school, Pete and Raymond followed Luke, who ______________________ (walk) to the trailer park.
3. Luke ___________________________ (smoke) a cigarette.
4. Pete and Raymond _____________________ (watch) him.



## ◯ Übung 27

*Beantworte die folgende Frage. Verwende dabei ein Verb im Past Continuous.*

What were Pete and Raymond doing on the ridge?

___________________________________________

___________________________________________

## ◯ Übung 28

*Welche Wörter passen hier? Die Buchstaben in den umrandeten Kästchen ergeben in der richtigen Reihenfolge wieder einen Namen.*

1. Pete wanted to let his father know what had
   _ _ _ _ _ □ _ _.

2. At first he didn't do it because he _ □ _ _ _ _ his father's anger.

3. But then he □ _ _ down with his father and
   _ □ _ _ him everything.

4. Mister Wilson □ _ _ _ _ to get angry.

5. But then he hugged his son and _ _ _ □ _ _ _ him for being honest.

Löungswort: □ □ □ □ □ □

# Drugs and detectives

Minutes went by, with Pete keeping an eye on the man and **monitoring** Raymond. In the distance, a car with a defective **muffler** droned closer. The fat man took his bag and walked slowly down the ridge to the parking spot. Pete covered Raymond's mouth with his hand, and as Ray awoke wide-eyed, he **motioned** his friend to keep quiet and pointed toward the street. Raymond nodded and looked down the **slope**.

The rust colored car that pulled into the parking area was far older than its driver. The fat man approached the car and handed his bag to the person inside, who paid with a large bundle of cash. With **squealing tires**, the car left the parking area and thundered to town.

**to monitor**: beaufsichtigen, bewachen
**muffler (am.) / silencer (brit.)**: Schalldämpfer
**to motion**: winken
**slope**: Böschung
**squealing**: quietschend
**tire (am.) / tyre (brit.)**: Reifen

Anna looked frightened as Pete told her the story. The two boys had waited a long time until the man was gone and had then silently left the forest and run all the way to town.

"And did you see Luke?" Anna wanted to know. They had forgotten about Luke. Both boys grinned **sheepishly** and shook their heads.

"Great detectives," Anna nodded. "So you don't know if the fat man has anything to do with Luke? They live next door, Luke's father does not have a job and the man you saw does cash business. He carries a gun at his home, he threatens to kill people. Maybe this is a case for the cops, Pete. Maybe we should start thinking like grown-ups."

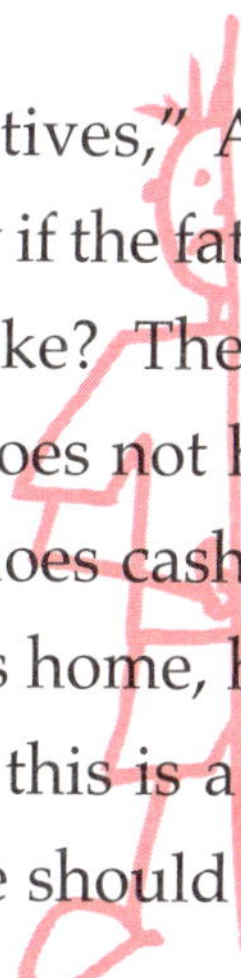

"You are absolutely right, Anna," Pete said **ruefully**. "My dad will be gone until tomorrow, but then we'll tell him what

**sheepishly**: verlegen
**ruefully**: reumütig

happened today."

Detective Wilson listened attentively. "Drugs," he **mumbled** and made a note.

"What you described certainly sounds like a typical drug deal."

"And the money, dad?"

"I am sure we will find it in the trailer. You kids helped us; I don't know if I should **scold** you for taking such risks or praise you for your investigative know-how. Maybe both," Mister Wilson grinned.



It had been a week since Pete and Raymond's adventure. They had taken turns following Luke into town and back toward his home, but none of them had wanted to go all the way to the trailer park. After school on Thursday, the band gathered in Pete's garage. It had been too long since they had practiced, and the first few songs were true garage quality; very bad and very loud.

**to mumble**: murmeln
**to scold**: tadeln

In the late afternoon, the long, black Lincoln had brought Benson and his keyboard. The chauffeur leaned against the garage wall and seemed to like what he heard. The kids were **flattered** to have an **audience**, but Benson had sent the driver home with a wave of his hand after the first song.

"You were not very polite, Benson," Anna said quietly after the man had left.

"Why should I be polite?" Benson asked surprised. "He is our chauffeur. He works for us."



Anna stared at him. She shook her head and began slapping her bass with the unmistakable opening **bars** of a lovely blues song. She played **doggedly**, kept up a droning bass line until the rest of the band fell in behind her. After the song, she unplugged, **stowed** her instrument in its

**to flatter**: schmeicheln
**audience**: Publikum, Zuschauer
**bar**: Takt
**doggedly**: verbissen, hartnäckig
**to stow**: verstauen

case and left without a word.

"What's up with her?" Benson wanted to know.

"I don't think you made the best **impression** on her today," Pete replied. "We have always tried to treat everyone with respect, and I believe she was **offended** by the way you treated your family chauffeur."

"Well," Benson shrugged, "**can't please them all**, I guess." The practice session ended with everyone quietly packing up and Benson **summoning** his driver on the cell phone.

"I thought you'd want to know that we got permission to take a closer look at the fat gentleman with all that money," Detective Wilson told his son over the dinner table. "The FBI had received a tip that **methamphetamine** was being sold there,



**impression**: Eindruck
**to offend**: ärgern
**can't please them all**: man kann es nicht jedem recht machen
**to summon**: rufen
**methamphetamine**: kristallines Amphetamin

and they sent us their information. My boss turned the investigation over to me. Without you, we would not have known. You did well, son."

Pete **glowed** with pride. Now, this was being a detective! Pete grinned so hard, he had difficulty **swallowing** his double decker cheeseburger. "Share the news with your two friends, but make sure it stays in your detective group," Mister Wilson said.



"This calls for a banana split," Anna stated, and after school the three of them headed for the **ice cream parlor**. They were in luck; the table in the corner was vacant. From there they had the best view of the street through dark green glass. Their giant banana splits were brought to the table, two whole bananas, halved and placed on oval plates, topped with **scoops** of ice cream, chocolate syrup, nuts and **mara-**

**to glow**: strahlen
**to swallow**: schlucken
**ice cream parlor (am.) / parlour (brit.)**: Eisdiele
**scoop**: Kugel

**schino cherries.**

"My parents would kill me if they knew how much sugar I'm eating today," Raymond grinned.

"Sure they would; but that only makes it taste even better," honest Anna knew.

"My dad says sugar makes me nervous," Raymond grinned. "Let's see how he likes me tonight, when I get home. I'll probably be zipping around the house like a balloon that's losing air."



"I will not be lying if I tell my dad we had an ice cream after school, will I?" Pete asked into the laughter at the table.

Anna had been **deep in thought** all day, and she finally spoke up. "We have to talk about Benson. There are a few things that do not feel right about him. I cannot **put my finger on it**, but I know that he is hiding something from us – or that he's

**maraschino cherry**: Maraschinokirsche (in Likör eingelegte Kirschen)
**deep in thought**: gedankenverloren
**to put my finger on it**: mit Sicherheit bestimmen

lying to us, which is even worse."

And then, Luke walked by. He threw a glance into the green ice cream parlor window, but the three friends knew he could not see them. He carried a painter's **canvas** under his arm, a bag **slung** over his shoulder, and the headphones he wore **deafened** him to the world.

## Short cut



*"Drogenhandel," sagt Detektiv Wilson, als Pete ihm seine Beobachtung schildert. Dass Benson ein arroganter Kerl ist, stört Anna, aber dass Petes Vater die Detektive lobt, geht herunter wie Öl. Oder eine Riesenportion Eis. Während die gelöffelt wird, spaziert Luke vorbei.*

**canvas**: Leinwand
**to sling**: werfen
**to deafen**: taub machen

## Übung 29

*1, 2 oder 3? Welches der drei Wörter passt? Die dazugehörigen Zahlen ergeben in der Summe 7.*

1. As a car approached, the fat man ☐ his bag and walked down to the parking spot.

   (1) had taken
   (2) took
   (3) is taking

2. He went to the car and ☐ his bag to the person inside.

   (1) was giving
   (2) has given
   (3) gave

3. This person ☐ him a large bundle of cash.

   (1) paid
   (2) is paying
   (3) has paid

4. Then the car ☐ the parking area.

   (1) left
   (2) leave
   (3) is leaving

Summe: ☐

## Übung 30

*Das Past Participle brauchst du auch, um das Past Perfect (Vorvergangenheit) zu bilden. Finde in diesem Suchrätsel das Past Participle der folgenden Verben:*

run: ______________ leave: ______________

go: ______________ forget: ______________

| | | | | | | |
|---|---|---|---|---|---|---|
| O | I | A | T | Z | K | F |
| L | B | R | O | F | W | O |
| H | A | R | L | L | P | R |
| L | E | F | T | A | T | G |
| Z | F | D | N | K | Z | O |
| S | I | R | Z | Y | E | T |
| E | K | N | E | E | K | T |
| R | T | U | G | O | N | E |
| Z | U | D | L | A | O | N |
| N | W | N | D | I | F | D |



## Übung 31

*Vervollständige nun die folgenden Sätze im Past Perfect.*

1. The fat man ____________________.
2. The boys ______ then ____________ the forest and ____________ to town.
3. They ______ completely ______________ about Luke.

## Übung 32

*Vervollständige die Bedingungssätze. Achte dabei auf die richtige Zeitform: Simple Past im if-Satz, would + Infinitiv im Hauptsatz.*

1. Pete said to Benson, "If you ________________ (treat) your chauffeur with respect, Anna ______________________________ (like) you."

2. Raymond grinned, "If my parents __________ (know) how much sugar I ate today, they ______________________________ (kill) me."



3. Pete replied, "My father ___________________ ___________ (not say) anything if I __________ (tell) him that we had an ice cream after school."

## Übung 33

*Rätsel! Welcher englische Begriff wird hier erklärt?*

This is a group of people who watch a football match or listen to a concert.

Lösung: ____________________________________

## Übung 34

*Welches der folgenden Wörter passt in welche Lücke?*

detective / gun / drugs / investigation / business

1. Pete told his father about the fat man whom they had watched doing cash ______________ and carrying a ______________.
2. Mister Wilson was told by the FBI that someone in the area dealt with ______________.
3. The FBI turned the ______________ over to him.
4. Mister Wilson allowed Pete to share the news with his ______________ friends.



## Übung 35

*Buchstabensalat! Um welches Wort handelt es sich hier?*

f-u-f-e-a-h-c-u-r: ______________________

"Check out his walk," Pete said. "He's listening to some great rock music, guaranteed."

Anna dropped her spoon. "I'm following him," she whispered loudly. "Wait here for me."

Not quite half an hour later, Pete's cell phone rang. "I followed him to an apartment house on Third Street. An old lady sat in a **rocker** on the **porch** next door, so I went over to ask her if she knew where the kid with the canvas under his arm went. She sits there from morning to night, knows everyone and everything on that street, and told me Luke goes there almost every day. The woman next door is his father's sister. She is an art teacher, and he takes lessons there. Seems he is quite the artist; she told me he had shown her a pic-



**rocker**: Schaukelstuhl
**porch (am.) / veranda (brit.)**: Veranda

ture he painted and it looked very professional."

"Stay there; I'll be with you in five minutes. We have to talk," Pete said. "Wait here for Benson," he asked Raymond, "and we will be back as soon as possible."

Anna waited for him at the corner of Main and Third. The two walked to the **fountain** in the small park and sat down on its **rim**.

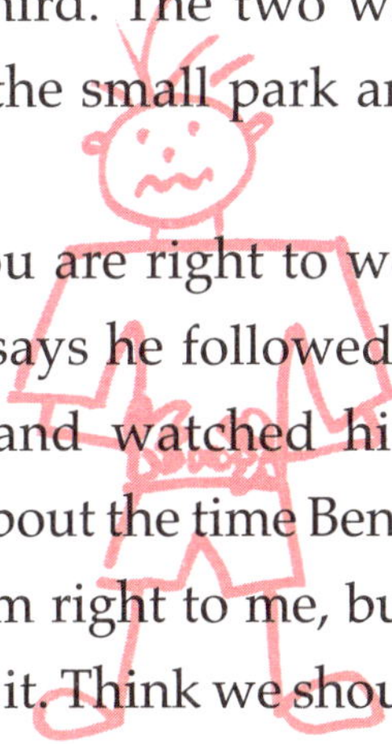

"Anna, you are right to wonder about Benson. He says he followed Luke to the gas station and watched him break in. Something about the time Benson saw him does not seem right to me, but I can´t put my finger on it. Think we should check out what Benson **has been up to**?"

Anna nodded. "I would feel badly about spying on Benson, but after his behavior toward the driver in your garage, I have



**fountain**: Springbrunnen
**rim**: Rand
**to be up to**: im Schilde führen

just lost all respect. He's no friend, and even if he were, I would not want him as a friend. We are much too different, and I don't feel comfortable around him."

"Me, too. I feel as though there's a lot we don't know about Benson."

"So," Anna declared, "let's get an **invitation** to visit our keyboard player at his fine home in the **expensive** part of town. Where people have chauffeurs they can treat like dogs and maybe even have secrets they can't hide from a couple of super **sleuths** like us."



Raymond called Pete at home. "Where were you? I sat there with Benson for an hour, listening to him **whine** about missing his friends in San Diego and how horrible Greenville is. I was about to **smack him one** when Luke walked by again. We

**invitation**: Einladung
**expensive**: teuer
**sleuth**: Detektiv, Spürhund
**to whine**: winseln
**to smack sb. one (ugs.)**: jdm. eine scheuern

followed him home. Nothing happened, though."

"Well," Pete said, "Anna and I had a couple of things to talk about. But if Benson feels so lonely here, how about calling him and asking him if we can't all come over to his house tomorrow afternoon? Maybe have a snack and do homework together? Think he would like that?"

"Sure," Raymond answered. "Let me give him a call. I'll see you at school tomorrow."



Boomer showed up at lunch again, but this time, he just stared at Pete as he walked by their table in the cafeteria.

"Wow," Anna said, **wiping her brow**. "Is he sick? No comment, no threat to beat us all to a pulp?"

"Shh, he might hear you," Pete warned. He was not at all convinced that Boomer had become a peacable fellow.

**to wipe one's brow**: sich über die Stirn fahren

Raymond was still out on the playing field. Tuesdays were his days for team sports, a class he hated with a **passion**. Anna and Pete finished their sandwiches and walked out of the cafeteria.

"I sat down last night and made a note of what had happened the last few days. And while doing that, something interesting **occurred to me**." Pete took her by the arm and steered her toward the far corner of the field.



"Remember when you returned to the trailer park? It must have been after ten. My dad left the house a few minutes before ten, I waited five minutes before leaving, and it took me about ten minutes to arrive at the trailer park. Raymond was there and complained he had been sitting under the tree for over two hours, in the dark and cold night."

"Of course," Anna said. "My parents

**passion**: Inbrunst
**to occure to sb.**: jdm. einfallen

always fall asleep during the Seinfeld show. I left when I heard my dad **snore**, around a quarter to ten."

"Right. And I saw Luke and his father, then the fat guy in the moonlight and you trying to get away. The moon shone straight down."

"I know," Anna said, "I saw his hairy arm as **clear as day**. That's why I hesitated before biting, because I was afraid I'd catch some horrible **bug** from the dirty guy."



"So we know it was past ten o'clock, closer to ten thirty, when all that happened. A few minutes before, Luke had taken care of his father and then left the trailer. But Benson told us he had left home when it got dark. Now, I checked the **almanac**; on my computer; Thursday, September the seventh, the sun set at 7:21pm here in Greenville. Benson told us he followed Luke to

**to snore**: schnarchen
**clear as day**: wie am helllichten Tag
**bug**: Bakterie
**almanac**: Almanach

town and watched him break into the gas station. He said he saw him clearly because Luke was wearing a white T-shirt and the moon, which had just risen, made the shirt shine in the dark. Well, the moon rose at 7:31 that evening. At ten o'clock, the moon **shone** straight down through the trees in the trailer park. Luke was in the trailer from around seven o'clock – the sun was **setting** as we followed him home, remember? – until he left after ten. Both Raymond and you and I watched the trailer until we had to go home, then Raymond took over and stayed there alone until I returned around ten. Luke could not have left and come back."



Anna had listened **wide-eyed**. She walked a circle, thinking.

"You're right," she said. "It's impossible. One of you is lying, and I know it is not

**to shine**: scheinen, strahlen
**to set**: untergehen
**wide-eyed**: mit großen Augen

you. Benson must be lying. I feel a lot better now about spying on Benson. A whole lot better."

When Pete, Raymond and Anna arrived at Benson's impressive **mansion**, the chauffeur was busy washing the town-car. He gave the kids a friendly wave as they approached.

"If it isn't the rock stars!" the man exclaimed. "I enjoyed your band."

The kids waved back. Pete rang the doorbell and a maid opened the door.

"Master Benson is in the living room, please follow me," she said.

Benson sat at a huge table, his science book open in front of him.

"Hi, have a seat. Juanita will bring us some snacks." He glanced at the maid, and she rushed off toward the kitchen.

"Nice house you have here," said Raymond.



**mansion**: Villa

"You should have seen our **place** in San Diego," Benson replied, "much bigger and nicer than this."

"Well, **it beats** the apartment I share with my parents," Raymond sighed.

"Benson, can I use your **restroom**?" Anna asked.

"Sure, upstairs, second door to the right."


Anna made her way up the stairs. The door to the room at the end of the hall had a poster of a popular rock band taped to it.

"This must be Benson's room," Anna thought to herself. She opened the door to the bathroom and closed it again, as if she had entered. Instead, she tiptoed toward Benson's room, and carefully opened the door.

His room was very large, and it seemed as if he owned every toy and **gadget** ever

**place (ugs.)**: Haus, Wohnung
**it beats (ugs.)**: besser als
**restroom (am.) / toilet (brit.)**: Badezimmer, Toilette
**gadget**: Gerät

invented. There was a big-screen television across from Benson's huge bed, and a brand-new computer sat on a desk. Anna opened the door to his **walk-in closet**, which was the size of her room at home. She **surveyed** the many clothes that hung inside and the dozens of tennis shoes neatly lined up in a row. Then Anna's eyes widened. She **fumbled** in her jacket pocket and retrieved the digital camera. Visibly excited, she took several pictures.



## Short cut

*Anna folgt Luke und stellt fest, dass er regelmäßig Kunstunterricht nimmt. Dass Benson lügt, hat Pete durch scharfsinnige Detektivarbeit herausbekommen. Den Beweis wollen die Detektive bei Benson zu Hause finden, wo Anna eine interessante Entdeckung macht.*

**walk-in closet (am.) / cupboard, wardrobe (brit.)**: großer Wandschrank
**to survey**: begutachten
**to fumble**: wühlen, suchen

# Übung 36

*Aus zwei mach eins! Verbinde die beiden Sätze mithilfe des Relativpronomens* ***who*** *oder* ***that****.*

1. Anna talked to an old woman. The old woman knew everyone and everything on that street.

   Anna talked to an old woman ______________

   ____________________________________________

   ____________________________________________

2. Luke went to see his aunt. His aunt was an art teacher.

   Luke went to ______________________________

   ____________________________________________

   ____________________________________________

3. Luke had shown the old woman a painting. The painting looked very professional.

   Luke had _________________________________

   ____________________________________________

   ____________________________________________

4. Pete asked Raymond to wait for Benson. Benson wanted to be back as soon as possible.

   Pete asked ________________________________

   ____________________________________________

   ____________________________________________

## Übung 37

*Kreuzworträtsel! Wie heißen die folgenden Wörter auf Englisch?*

1. Villa
2. Flur
3. Badezimmer
4. Wohnung
5. Küche
6. Kleiderschrank

## Übung 38

*1, 2 oder 3? Welche der drei Verbformen passt? Die dazugehörigen Zahlen ergeben in der Summe 9.*

*Tipp: Es muss jedesmal das Past Continuous verwendet werden!*

1. Benson said he recognized Luke at the gas station because the moon ☐ .

   (1) was shining
   (2) is shining
   (3) shines



2. According to Benson, Luke ☐ a white T-shirt.

   (1) were wearing
   (2) is wearing
   (3) was wearing

3. But Pete said that Luke was at the trailer park where he and Raymond ☐ him.

   (1) watched
   (2) was watching
   (3) were watching

4. Anna said that one of the boys ☐ .

   (1) is lying
   (2) was lying
   (3) lied

Summe: ☐

## Übung 39

*Welche Wörter passen hier? Die Buchstaben in den umrandeten Kästchen ergeben in der richtigen Reihenfolge wieder einen Namen.*

1. The kids decided to go to Benson's house and do their _ □ _ _ _ _ _ _ _ together.

2. Benson was already □ _ _ _ _ _ _ for them in the living room.

3. Anna asked him if she could use the _ _ □ _ _ _ _ _.

4. But she went to have a look at Benson's room and opened his walk-in _ □ _ _ _ _.

5. She saw dozens of _ _ □ _ _ _ shoes.

6. She took several _ □ _ _ _ _ _ _ _ with her digital camera.

Lösungswort: □ □ □ □ □ □

## Caught red-handed

"Are you lost?"

Startled, Anna almost dropped the camera.

"Can I help you, Miss?" the maid wanted to know.

Anna thought for a moment. "I, I think I am lost. I am looking for the bathroom."



"This way." The maid pointed down the hall. Anna **brushed past** the woman and entered the bathroom. She waited several minutes before returning downstairs.

"We thought you fell in," chuckled Benson. Anna blushed.

"Hey, look!" Pete yelled as he pointed at the television set. The local news showed the trailer park, then the fat man being led away in handcuffs. Pete's dad was telling a reporter how they had found a methamphetamine laboratory inside the fat man's

**caught red-handed**: auf frischer Tat ertappt
**to brush past**: streifen

trailer, along with a large sum of cash. "I couldn't have caught these dangerous criminals without the help of my son and his group of detectives. They deserve all the credit."

The kids jumped with joy, exchanging **high-fives**.

Benson sat at the table, a **grim** look on his face. "What about Luke's part in all of this? Nobody mentioned him."

"I'm not feeling so good. I think I will go home." Anna placed one hand on her stomach.

"I guess we should be going as well," Raymond said to Pete, who nodded in agreement.

"Let's get back to the garage, I have to show you something," Anna said as the kids hurried down the street. "You won't believe your eyes."



**high-fives (ugs., am.)**: händeklatschende Freudengeste
**grim**: finster

Anna connected the camera to her laptop and began downloading the afternoon's pictures. Pete and Raymond stared at the computer screen with great **anticipation**. Their excitement turned to disappointment as they saw the photos.

"What is so great about a **bunch** of shoes?" Raymond muttered.

"Take a closer look," Anna replied as she zoomed in on a pair of tennis shoes.



"**Holy Moly**!" Pete yelled as he got closer to the screen.

The shoes were covered with tiny specks of purple paint.

"Son, I'm afraid this evidence will not hold up in court."

Mister Wilson handed the photos back to his son. "However, it makes Benson our main suspect."

"How do we prove it's him breaking in

**anticipation**: Erwartung
**bunch (ugs., am.) / lot (brit.)**: Haufen
**Holy Moly**: Heiliger Bimbam

and vandalizing property?" Pete asked.

"**Catch him in the act,**" Detective Wilson suggested.

"And how do we do that?" Anna wanted to know.

"Benson seems to be a **bold** kid who thinks he is superior to us," Raymond suggested. "I believe he would be willing to take a risk in order to prove how smart he is."



Pete thought for a moment. "What if we were to organize a concert at the community center?"

Mister Wilson and the kids listened **attentively**.

"We could call it Music against Vandalism," Pete continued, "and if Benson is as bold as we think he is, he will show up and **leave his mark**."

"Great idea!" Anna was excited. "But

**to catch in the act**: auf frischer Tat ertappen
**bold**: dreist
**attentively**: aufmerksam
**to leave his mark**: Zeichen hinterlassen

how will a concert help us catch Benson?"

Pete looked at his dad. "The Greenville Police Department has some great new video equipment, right, dad?"

"Right, son. And I can use it to monitor the community center for a few days."

Pete **beamed**. "If someone comes in and sprays his graffiti, we will have him on video tape. And that will **hold up in court**, right, dad?"



"Exactly," Mister Wilson said. "Great plan, kids. I will call Mister Jones at the community center."

"We can make flyers and hand them out at school!" Pete offered.

ROCK AGAINST VANDALISM read the flyer that Anna proudly presented to her friends. She had even included a photo of the band in action. The flyer **encouraged** kids to attend the free concert this

**to beam**: strahlen
**to hold up in court**: Beweiskraft vor Gericht haben
**to encourage**: ermutigen

coming Sunday.

Pete **patted** Anna on the back. "Good job!"

"Look who is coming," Raymond whispered.

Benson approached the kids and pointed at the flyer. "Cool, next Sunday then?"

The kids nodded. It was hard for them to **conceal** their **suspicion**.

On Pete's way to school on Friday morning, he saw Boomer across the street.

"Wilson, I want to talk to you." Boomer had a serious look on his face.

Pete wanted to run, but the bully was too close and would surely catch him. Pete imagined himself on stage Sunday, with two **shiners** and a missing tooth.

The boy put his hand on Pete's shoulder. "I want to thank you."

Pete stared at Boomer in disbelief. This



**to pat**: tätscheln
**to conceal**: verbergen
**suspicion**: Argwohn, Verdacht
**shiner (ugs.)**: blaues Auge

must be a trick, he thought and took a step back.

"My brother," Boomer began. "He is addicted to **crystal meth**. Your father made him join a **recovery** program. He will now get the help he needs."

Pete saw tears in the boy's eyes. "I'm glad my dad could help him. Maybe we will see you on Sunday at the concert?"

Boomer nodded.



On Sunday, Pete woke up to his father's car pulling up in front of the house.

"Bingo!" Detective Wilson said. "Call Anna and Raymond and tell them to meet us at the police station."

The black and white video on the screen showed the **rear** stage wall at the community center. A person dressed in black appeared. The kids watched wide-eyed as the figure on the screen covered the wall

**crystal meth (ugs.)**: gefährliche, leicht herzustellende Droge, auch "Ice", "Crank", „Speed"
**recovery**: Gesundung
**rear**: hinterer Teil

with spray paint. Then the culprit turned toward the camera, and the detectives saw the grin on Benson's face.

"We knew it!" Pete snapped his fingers. "Now what, dad?"

"Now we wait. I have already sent a **squad car** to pick up Benson at home."

Benson sat at a table next to his father when Detective Wilson and the kids entered the **interrogation** room.



"Why did you do it?" Pete asked.

"Maybe I just wanted to prove that I can get away with it," Benson replied **smugly.**

Benson's father turned to his son. "How could you **embarrass** me like this? My son, a common criminal?"

"I hate it here. I hate the new school, I miss my friends in San Diego, and you dad, you just care about yourself. All you do is work, we never spend any time together."

**squad car**: Streifenwagen
**interrogation**: Vernehmung
**smugly**: selbstgefällig
**to embarrass**: blamieren

Benson turned to the kids. "Being part of your group was like a game for me. You suspected Luke even though the real culprit was right under your noses," the boy said proudly.

Anna leaned over the table and said angrily, "You took advantage of us. You wanted Luke to **be blamed for something** with which he had nothing to do. I understand that you are unhappy, but that is no excuse."



Benson looked over at Mister Wilson. "May I go home now?"

The detective nodded. "You may go with your father. You are not to leave the house. We will be in touch."

"Sad, but I still can't get over the fact that he would be so **two-faced**," Anna said after Benson had gone.

"Let's pack our stuff. The concert begins

**to blame sb. for sth.**: jdm. die Schuld an etwas geben
**two-faced**: falsch, heuchlerisch

in a few hours!" Pete **urged.**

The curtain opened. A hundred kids fell silent as they saw the huge, fresh graffiti on the wall behind the stage.

Pete stepped up to the microphone. "Hi all, thanks for coming and supporting Rock against Vandalism! This is the last graffiti – the vandal has been caught." The audience applauded while someone drew the rear curtain over Benson's work. The spotlights clicked on and the band launched into "Smoke On The Water".



A **lanky** youth with a bright red Stratocaster guitar walked on the stage. "Luke?" Anna could not believe her eyes. He grinned, plugged in and joined the band.

## Short cut

*Anna findet Beweise für Bensons Schuld. Detektiv Wilson hilft den Kids, den Graffitisprüher dingfest zu machen.*

**to urge**: drängen
**lanky**: schlaksig

## Übung 40

*Setze die folgenden Sätze ins Passiv.*

1. The local news showed the trailer park.

______________________________________

______________________________________

2. A police officer led the fat man away in handcuffs.

______________________________________

______________________________________



3. The police had found drugs in the fat man's trailer.

______________________________________

______________________________________

4. The police caught the drug dealers thanks to Pete and his friends.

______________________________________

______________________________________

5. The kids caught Benson in the act.

______________________________________

______________________________________

## Übung 41

*Suche in diesem Rätsel die englische Übersetzung der folgenden Verben:*

wissen – ____________________
zeigen – ____________________
erwähnen – ____________________
nicken – ____________________
fragen – ____________________
vorschlagen – ____________________
denken – ____________________
zuhören – ____________________



*Tipp: Du findest alle diese Wörter im letzten Kapitel!*

| | | | | | | | |
|---|---|---|---|---|---|---|---|
| K | E | L | D | Z | U | K | A |
| E | N | E | S | T | G | I | W |
| C | I | O | T | A | R | L | E |
| A | Y | S | W | O | O | I | N |
| M | A | L | C | L | P | S | T |
| S | U | G | G | E | S | T | A |
| C | O | U | L | D | Z | E | T |
| S | X | B | A | I | T | N | E |
| M | K | N | S | S | K | E | D |
| E | Q | U | K | V | A | F | U |
| N | W | F | L | I | F | T | P |
| T | Y | T | H | I | N | K | H |
| I | D | A | F | E | Q | O | J |
| O | F | X | S | H | O | W | I |
| N | A | D | E | T | K | A | S |
| D | S | A | I | D | N | O | D |

## ◯ Übung 42

*Pete und seine Freunde besprechen, wie sie Benson auf frischer Tat ertappen können. Vervollständige die folgenden Bedingungssätze. Achte dabei wieder auf die richtige Zeitform: Simple Present im if-Satz, will-Future im Hauptsatz.*

1. "If Benson ________________________ (be) as bold as we think, he ________________________ (show) up at the show and spray graffiti once more."



2. "If he ____________________________ (come) in and ________________________ (spray) his graffiti, we ____________________________ (have) him on video tape."

3. "If we _________________________ (have) him on video tape, this evidence ______________________ (hold) up in court."

## ◯ Übung 43

*Buchstabensalat! Um welches englische Wort handelt es sich hier?*

a-l-v-m-s-i-a-d-n: ________________________________

# Übung 44

*Welches der folgenden Wörter passt in welche Lücke?*

saw / caught / applauded / decided / handed / called

1. The kids ______________________ to organize a concert.

2. They ______________________ it Rock against Vandalism.

3. Anna made a flyer that the kids _____________ out at school.

4. At the concert, the audience ________________ the huge, fresh graffiti on the wall.

5. Pete told the audience that it was the last graffiti because the vandal had been ______________.

6. The audience ___________________, and the band launched into "Smoke On The Water".

# Lösungen



**Übung 1:**
1. solved 2. spent 3. was 4. introduced 5. broken
**Übung 2:** 1. detectives 2. teacher 3. bully
**Übung 4:** 1. rock band 2. garage 3. bass guitar 4. drums 5. school
Lösungswort: Boomer
**Übung 5:**
1. Pete's father was a detective **who** had done a great job raising his son.
2. Benson was a shy boy **who** moved there from San Diego.
3. Luke was a skinny kid **who** wore torn jeans and a T-shirt.
**Übung 6:**
1. The store's side door **was forced** open.
2. A lot of bottles **were broken**.
3. Graffiti **were sprayed** on the walls.
**Übung 7:**
The dark building **was illuminated** by the emergency lights of the police car.
**Übung 9:**
1. had broken 2. had sprayed 3. had … vandalized 4. had done
**Übung 10:**
A bully.
**Übung 11:**
1. investigating (2) 2. keep (1) 3. saw (3) 4. classmate (3)
**Übung 12:**
1. was snoring 2. was trying 3. was drawing 4. were paying 5. was ... stealing; vandalizing
**Übung 14:**
1. decipher 2. digital 3. impressed 4. smart; great
**Übung 15:**
homework assignment
**Übung 16:**
1. doesn't leave; will be 2. play; will be 3. don't stop; will be
**Übung 17:**
1. had found 2. had taken 3. had been
**Übung 18:**
A notebook.

**Übung 20:**
1. who 2. that 3. who 4. that 5. who 6. who
**Übung 21:**
1. thrown (2) 2. stumbled (1) 3. drunk (3) 4. helped (2)
**Übung 22:**
1. see; will kill 2. will not be / won't be; have
3. makes; will find
**Übung 23:**
graffiti
**Übung 25:**
1. broken 2. sprayed 3. seen
**Übung 26:**
1. was talking 2. was walking 3. was smoking
4. were watching
**Übung 27:**
They were waiting for Luke to return.
**Übung 28:**
1. happened 2. feared 3. sat; told 4. began 5. thanked
Lösungswort: Benson
**Übung 29:**
1. took (2) 2. gave (3) 3. paid (1) 4. left (1)
**Übung 31:**
1. had gone 2. had … left; run 3. had … forgotten
**Übung 32:**
1. treated; would like 2. knew; would kill
3. wouldn't say; told
**Übung 33:**
An audience.
**Übung 34:**
1. business; gun 2. drugs 3. investigation 4. detective
**Übung 35:**
chauffeur
**Übung 36:**
1. Anna talked to an old woman who knew everyone and everything on that street.
2. Luke went to see his aunt who was an art teacher.
3. Luke had shown the old woman a painting that looked very professional.
4. Pete asked Raymond to wait for Benson who wanted to be back as soon as possible.

**Übung 38:**

1. was shining (1) 2. was wearing (3) 3. were watching (3)
4. was lying (2)

**Übung 39:**

1. homework 2. waiting 3. restroom 4. closet 5. tennis
6. pictures

Lösungswort: Wilson

**Übung 40:**

1. The trailer park was shown in the local news.
2. The fat man was led away in handcuffs (by a police officer).
3. Drugs had been found in the fat man's trailer (by the police).
4. The drug dealers were caught thanks to Pete and his friends.
5. Benson was caught in the act (by the kids).

**Übung 42:**

1. is; will show 2. comes; sprays; will have 3. have; will hold

**Übung 43:**

vandalism

**Übung 44:**

1. decided 2. called 3. handed 4. saw 5. caught
6. applauded

**Übung 3:**

| | | | | | | | |
|---|---|---|---|---|---|---|---|
| H | E | L | D | | | | |
| | | | | | | | |
| | | | | | | | |
| | | S | T | O | O | D | |
| | | | | | | | |
| | | | | | | | A |
| C | O | U | L | D | | | T |
| | | | | | | | E |
| | | | | S | | | |
| | | | | | A | | |
| | | | | | | T | |
| | | | | L | | O | |
| S | | | | E | | O | |
| A | | | | F | | K | |
| I | | | | T | | | |
| D | | | | | | | |

**Übung 8:**

| | | | | | | | | | | | | |
|---|---|---|---|---|---|---|---|---|---|---|---|---|
| | | | | | | 4 | | | | | | |
| | | | | | | I | | | | | | |
| 1 | R | E | S | P | O | N | D | | | | | |
| | | | | | | V | | | | | | 6 |
| | | | | | 2 | E | X | P | L | A | I | N |
| | | | | | | S | | | | | | O |
| | | | | | | T | | 5 | | | | T |
| | | | | | | I | | W | | | | I |
| | | | | | 3 | G | U | A | R | D | | C |
| | | | | | | A | | R | | | | E |
| | | | | | | T | | N | | | | |
| | | | | | | E | | | | | | |

## Übung 13:

| | | | | | | | |
|---|---|---|---|---|---|---|---|
| H | I | D | | | | | T |
| | | | | | | | H |
| | | | | | | | O |
| | | | K | | | | U |
| W | O | K | E | | | | G |
| | | | P | | R | | H |
| | | | T | | A | | T |
| | | | | | N | | |
| | | | | | G | | |
| | | C | | | | | |
| M | | | A | | | | |
| | E | | | U | | | |
| | | T | | | G | | |
| | | | | | | H | |
| | | | | | | | T |
| D | R | E | W | | | | |

## Übung 19:

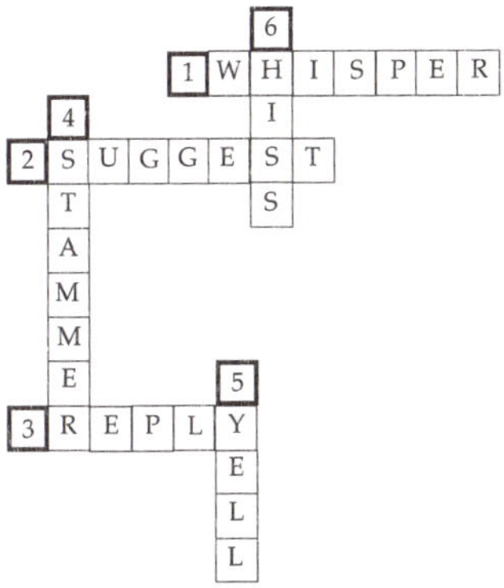


## Übung 24:

| | | | | | | |
|---|---|---|---|---|---|---|
| | | | | | | |
| | B | | | | | |
| | | R | | | | |
| | | | O | | | |
| | | | | K | | |
| S | P | R | A | Y | E | D |
| E | | | | | | N |
| E | | | | | | |
| N | | | | | | |

## Übung 30:

| | | | | | | |
|---|---|---|---|---|---|---|
| | | | | | | F |
| | | | | | | O |
| | | | | | | R |
| L | E | F | T | | | G |
| | | | | | | O |
| | | | | | | T |
| | | | | | | T |
| R | | | G | O | N | E |
| | U | | | | | N |
| | | N | | | | |



## Übung 37:

## Übung 41:

| | | | | | | | |
|---|---|---|---|---|---|---|---|
| K | | | | | | | |
| | N | | | | | | |
| | | O | | | | L | |
| | | | W | | | I | |
| | | | | | | S | |
| S | U | G | G | E | S | T | |
| | | | | | | E | |
| | | | A | | | N | |
| M | | | S | | | | |
| E | | | K | | | | |
| N | | | | | | | |
| T | | T | H | I | N | K | |
| I | | | | | | | |
| O | | | S | H | O | W | |
| N | | | | | | | |
| | | | | | N | O | D |

## Relativsätze (*Relative Clauses*)

Mit Hilfe von Relativsätzen kannst du ein vorangegangenes Nomen – z.B. eine Person, ein Tier oder einen Gegenstand – näher beschreiben. Du kannst also im gleichen Satz zusätzliche Informationen liefern, ohne das Nomen noch einmal wiederholen zu müssen.

Aus diesen beiden Sätzen kannst du ein Satzgefüge mit einem Relativsatz bilden:



*Pete's father was a detective. The detective had raised his son alone.*

*Pete's father was a detective **who had raised his son alone**.*
Petes Vater war ein Kriminalbeamter, **der seinen Sohn allein großgezogen hatte**.

Einen Relativsatz bildest du, indem du das Nomen, das näher bestimmt wird, durch ein Relativpronomen (*who* oder *that*) ersetzt.

**Aufgepasst**: Das Verb steht in einem englischen Relativsatz, genauso wie im Hauptsatz, an zweiter Stelle, also direkt nach dem Relativpronomen *who* oder *that*!

### Relativpronomen: *who oder that?*

Bei der Wahl des richtigen Relativpronomens musst du im Englischen nur darauf achten, ob es um eine Person oder um eine Sache geht.

Bei Personen verwendest du das Relativpronomen *who*.

> *Luke was **a** poor, skinny **boy who** lived in a trailer park.*
> Luke war **ein** armer, magerer **Junge**, **der** in einem Wohnwagenpark lebte.

Bei Gegenständen oder Sachen (und bei Tieren) verwendest du das Relativpronomen *that*.

> *Anna made **a flyer that** the kids handed out at school.*
> Anna gestaltete **einen Flyer**, **den** die Jugendlichen in der Schule verteilten.



## Relativsätze ohne Relativpronomen

Im Englischen gibt es auch Relativsätze, bei denen das Relativpronomen einfach weggelassen werden kann. Das Relativpronomen kann immer dann weggelassen werden, wenn es **Objekt** des Relativsatzes ist.

Anstelle von:

> *The flyer **that** the kids handed out at school had been made by Anna.*
> Der Flyer, den die Jugendlichen in der Schule verteilten, war von Anna gestaltet worden.

kannst du auch schreiben:

> *The flyer the kids handed out at school had been made by Anna.*

# Bedingungssätze
# (*Conditional Sentences*)

Mit Hilfe von Bedingungssätzen kannst du ausdrücken, was passiert, wenn eine bestimmte Bedingung erfüllt wird.

In Bedingungssätzen steht im Englischen immer die Konjunktion *if* (= wenn, falls).
Jeder Bedingungssatz besteht aus einem *if*-Satz und einem Hauptsatz:

> *If the kids find the culprit, Pete's father will be happy.*
> Wenn die Kinder den Täter finden, wird Petes Vater sich freuen.



Es gibt unterschiedliche Typen von Bedingungssätzen:

Bedingungssatz I

Wenn du dir **sicher** bist, dass etwas Bestimmtes geschehen wird, wenn die Bedingung erfüllt wird, musst du einen Bedingungssatz des Typs I verwenden.

> *If the weather is nice, I'll go to the swimming-pool.*
> Wenn das Wetter schön ist, werde ich ins Schwimmbad gehen.

Bedingungssatz II

Wenn du es für **unwahrscheinlich** oder sogar für **unmöglich** hältst, dass eine Bedingung erfüllt wird, musst du einen Bedingungssatz des Typs II verwenden.

> *If I had a lot of money, I would travel around the world.*
> Wenn ich viel Geld hätte, würde ich eine Weltreise machen.

## Formen

Bedingungssatz I

Im *if*-Satz steht das *Simple Present*, im Hauptsatz das Futur (*will-Future*).



> *If Pete* ***finds*** *the culprit, the police* ***will arrest*** *him.*
> Wenn Pete den Täter findet, wird die Polizei ihn festnehmen.

Bedingungssatz II

Im *if*-Satz steht das *Simple Past*, im Hauptsatz *would* + Infinitiv.

> *If Benson* ***was*** *the culprit, he* ***would*** *never* ***admit*** *it.*
> Wenn Benson der Täter wäre, würde er dies nie zugeben.

**Beachte**: Wenn der *if*-Satz am Anfang steht, wird zwischen *if*-Satz und Hauptsatz immer ein Komma gesetzt. Wenn aber der Hauptsatz an erster Stelle steht, darfst du vor dem *if*-Satz kein Komma setzen!

# Das Passiv

Das Passiv verwendest du, wenn du betonen möchtest, was mit dem Subjekt getan wird. Dabei steht im Mittelpunkt, **was** getan wird und nicht **wer** dies tut.

> *The drug dealer was arrested.*
> Der Drogenhändler wurde festgenommen.

Wichtig ist hier, dass der Drogenhändler **festgenommen wurde**, nicht **wer** ihn festnahm.



Möchtest du aber doch erwähnen, wer für die Handlung verantwortlich ist, verwendest du die Präposition *by*.

> *The drug dealer was arrested* ***by the police****.*
> Der Drogenhändler wurde **von der Polizei** festgenommen.

Um das Passiv zu bilden, brauchst du immer zwei Teile:
- eine Form des Verbs *be*
- das *Past Participle*

Das *Past Participle* bildest du bei regelmäßigen Verben, indem du ***-ed*** ans Verb anhängst:
z.B. *play* → *play**ed***, *interrupt* → *interrupt**ed***, *arrest* → *arrest**ed***

Bei allen unregelmäßigen Verben musst du das *Past Participle* auswendig lernen:
z.B. *drive* → *driven*, *see* → *seen*, *find* → *found*, *take* → *taken*

## Zeitformen

Das Passiv gibt es in denselben Zeiten wie das Aktiv. Folgende Zeitformen werden am häufigsten verwendet:

*Simple Present* (Einfache Gegenwart):

*am / is / are + Past Participle*

> *Drug dealers* ***are arrested*** *almost every day.*
> Fast jeden Tag werden Drogenhändler festgenommen.

*Simple Past* (Einfache Vergangenheit):

*was / were + Past Participle*

> *The man* ***was led*** *away in handcuffs.*
> Der Mann wurde in Handschellen abgeführt.



*Past Perfect* (Vorvergangenheit):

*had been + Past Participle*

> *Luke* ***had been seen*** *at the gas station.*
> Luke war an der Tankstelle gesehen worden.

*Future* (Zukunft):

*will be + Past Participle*

> *The culprit* ***will be arrested****!*
> Der Täter wird festgenommen werden!

# Die Vorvergangenheit (*Past Perfect*)

Du verwendest das *Past Perfect* (Vorvergangenheit oder auch Plusquamperfekt), wenn du ausdrücken möchtest, dass ein Ereignis **vor** einem bestimmten Zeitpunkt in der Vergangenheit stattgefunden hat.

> *When the kids arrived at school, they saw that someone* ***had sprayed graffiti on the walls****.*
> Als die Kinder ins Schulgebäude kamen, sahen sie, dass jemand die Wände mit Graffiti besprüht hatte.



Die Graffiti wurden also gesprüht, **bevor** die Kinder ins Schulgebäude kamen.

Um das *Past Perfect* zu bilden, brauchst du immer zwei Teile:

- *had*
- *Past Participle*

z.B. *had eaten, had shown, had interrupted, had played*

Das *Past Participle* bildest du bei regelmäßigen Verben, indem du ***-ed*** ans Verb anhängst:
z.B. *arrive → arriv**ed**, arrest → arrest**ed**, talk → talk**ed***

Bei allen unregelmäßigen Verben musst du das *Past Participle* auswendig lernen:
z.B. *say → said, see → seen, find → found, take → taken*

## *Past Perfect* oder *Simple Past*?

| | |
|---|---|
| *When Luke **arrived**,*<br>Als Luke ankam,<br><br>*Benson **accused** Luke*<br>Benson beschuldigte Luke,<br><br>*The kids **arrived** at the community center*<br>Die Kinder kamen im Gemeindezentrum an, | *class **had** already **started**.*<br>hatte der Unterricht schon begonnen.<br><br>*because he **had seen** him at the gas station.*<br>weil er ihn an der Tankstelle gesehen hatte.<br><br>*after Benson **had sprayed** graffiti.*<br>nachdem Benson Graffiti gesprüht hatte. |
| ↓<br>Dies geschah zu einem bestimmten Zeitpunkt in der Vergangenheit. | ↓<br>Dies geschah noch **vor** diesem Zeitpunkt. |
| ↓<br>Hier verwendest du das ***Simple Past***. | ↓<br>Hier verwendest du das ***Past Perfect***. |

# Die Vergangenheit in Erzählungen (*Simple Past* und *Past Progressive*)

Beim Lesen des Krimis sind dir vor allem die beiden folgenden Vergangenheitsformen begegnet: das *Simple Past* (Einfache Vergangenheit) und das *Past Continuous* oder *Past Progressive* (Verlaufsform der Vergangenheit).

## *Simple Past*

Das *Simple Past* bildest du bei regelmäßigen Verben, indem du ***-ed*** an das Verb anhängst: z.B. *talk* → *talk**ed***.

Bei unregelmäßigen Verben musst du das *Simple Past* auswendig lernen: z.B. *see* → *saw*.

Das *Simple Past* sieht in allen Personen gleich aus: z.B. *I talked, he talked, they talked*.

## *Past Progressive*

Das *Past Progressive* besteht aus zwei Teilen:

- *was / were*
- Verb in der *ing*-Form

| | | |
|---|---|---|
| *I*<br>*he / she / it* | *was* | *talking* |
| *you / we / they* | *were* | *talking* |

## *Simple Past* oder *Past Progressive?*

Normalerweise werden Ereignisse, die in der Vergangenheit stattfanden, im ***Simple Past*** erzählt:

> *Anna **drew** a camera out of her bag and **took** some photos.*
> Anna nahm einen Fotoapparat aus ihrer Tasche und machte einige Fotos.

Das ***Past Progressive*** beschreibt einen Vorgang, der zu einem bestimmten Zeitpunkt in der Vergangenheit bereits im Gange war bzw. länger andauerte:

> *Anna **was talking** to her friends when suddenly Benson arrived.*
> Anna unterhielt sich gerade mit ihren Freunden, als plötzlich Benson auftauchte.

Vorgang A (Anna unterhält sich mit ihren Freunden) war bereits im Gange, als Vorgang B (Benson taucht auf) eintrat.

Außerdem wird das ***Past Progressive*** in Erzählungen oft verwendet, um eine Situation oder eine Szene zu beschreiben, in der etwas geschah:

> *The students **were sitting** in the classroom. Their teacher **was talking** about some historical event. Most kids **were listening** to the teacher, others **were drawing** on their notebooks or **dreaming**. Suddenly the door **opened** and …*

## Unregelmäßige Verben



| | |
|---|---|
| **be, was, been:** | sein |
| **beat, beat, beaten:** | schlagen |
| **become, became, become:** | werden |
| **begin, began, begun:** | beginnen |
| **bite, bit, bitten:** | beißen |
| **bleed, bled, bled:** | bluten |
| **blow, blew, blown:** | blasen |
| **break, broke, broken:** | brechen, zerbrechen |
| **bring, brought, brought:** | bringen |
| **build, built, built:** | bauen |
| **buy, bought, bought:** | kaufen |
| **can, could, –:** | können |
| **catch, caught, caught:** | fangen |
| **choose, chose, chosen:** | auswählen |
| **come, came, come:** | kommen |
| **cost, cost, cost:** | kosten |
| **cut, cut, cut:** | schneiden |
| **do, did, done:** | tun, machen |
| **draw, drew, drawn:** | zeichnen |
| **drink, drank, drunk:** | trinken |
| **drive, drove, driven:** | fahren |
| **eat, ate, eaten:** | essen |
| **fall, fell, fallen:** | fallen |
| **feed, fed, fed:** | füttern |
| **feel, felt, felt:** | fühlen |
| **fly, flew, flown:** | fliegen |
| **forget, forgot, forgotten:** | vergessen |
| **get, got, got:** | bekommen |
| **give, gave, given:** | geben |
| **go, went, gone:** | gehen |
| **grow, grew, grown:** | wachsen |
| **hang, hung, hung:** | hängen |
| **have, had, had:** | haben |
| **hear, heard, heard:** | hören |

| | |
|---|---|
| **hide, hid, hidden:** | verstecken |
| **hit, hit, hit:** | schlagen |
| **hold, held, held:** | halten |
| **hurt, hurt, hurt:** | verletzen, wehtun |
| **keep, kept, kept:** | behalten |
| **know, knew, known:** | wissen |
| **learn, learnt, learnt:** | lernen |
| **let, let, let:** | lassen |
| **lie, lay, lain:** | liegen |
| **lose, lost, lost:** | verlieren |
| **make, made, made:** | machen |
| **mean, meant, meant:** | meinen, bedeuten |
| **meet, met, met:** | treffen |
| **pay, paid, paid:** | bezahlen |
| **put, put, put:** | setzen, stellen, legen |
| **read, read, read:** | lesen |
| **ride, rode, ridden:** | reiten |
| **ring, rang, rung:** | klingeln |
| **run, ran, run:** | rennen |
| **say, said, said:** | sagen |
| **see, saw, seen:** | sehen |
| **sell, sold, sold:** | verkaufen |
| **send, sent, sent:** | schicken |
| **sing, sang, sung:** | singen |
| **sink, sank, sunk:** | sinken |
| **sit, sat, sat:** | sitzen |
| **sleep, slept, slept:** | schlafen |
| **speak, spoke, spoken:** | sprechen |
| **stand, stood, stood:** | stehen |
| **steal, stole, stolen:** | stehlen |
| **swim, swam, swum:** | schwimmen |
| **take, took, taken:** | nehmen |
| **think, thought, thought:** | denken |
| **understand, understood, understood:** | verstehen |
| **win, won, won:** | gewinnen |

# Vokabelverzeichnis

| | |
|---|---|
| **according**: | gemäß, nach, laut |
| **account**: | Bericht |
| **almanac**: | Almanach |
| **amid**: | inmitten |
| **anticipation**: | Erwartung |
| **attentively**: | aufmerksam |
| **audience**: | Publikum, Zuschauer |
| **backyard**: | Garten (am.) / Hinterhof (brit.) |
| **bar**: | Takt |
| **(to) beam**: | strahlen |
| **bear hug**: | kräftige Umarmung |
| **(to) beat sb. to a pulp (ugs.)**: | jdn. zu Brei schlagen |
| **(to) be up to**: | im Schilde führen |
| **bite mark**: | Bisswunde |
| **(to) blame sb. for sth.**: | jdm. die Schuld an etwas geben |
| **(to) blush**: | erröten |
| **bold**: | dreist |
| **(to) bolt out**: | hinausstürzen |
| **booze (ugs.)**: | Fusel |
| **(to) bow**: | sich verbeugen |
| **brat**: | freches Kind |
| **(to) brush past**: | streifen |
| **buddy (am.) / chum (brit.)**: | Kumpel |
| **bug**: | Bakterie |
| **bully**: | brutaler Kerl |
| **bunch (ugs., am.) / lot (brit.)**: | Haufen |
| **(to) burst out laughing**: | in Gelächter ausbrechen |
| **(to) buzz**: | summen |

| | |
|---|---|
| **can:** | Dose |
| **can't please them all:** | man kann es nicht jedem recht machen |
| **canvas:** | Leinwand |
| **(to) catch in the act:** | auf frischer Tat ertappen |
| **caught red-handed:** | auf frischer Tat ertappt |
| **(to) chat:** | plaudern |
| **(to) choke:** | würgen |
| **chrome-barreled (am.) / barrelled (brit.):** | mit verchromtem Lauf |
| **chubby:** | rundlich |
| **chuckle:** | Kichern |
| **clear as day:** | wie am helllichten Tag |
| **cliffhanger:** | spannende Sache |
| **(to) conceal:** | verbergen |
| **(to) crawl:** | kriechen |
| **crooked:** | schief |
| **(to) crush:** | zerdrücken |
| **crystal meth (ugs.):** | gefährliche, leicht herzustellende Droge |
| **culprit:** | Täter |
| **curb (am.) / kerb (brit.):** | Bordstein |
| **curfew:** | Ausgangsverbot |
| **currently:** | zur Zeit |
| **cute:** | niedlich |
| **(to) dare:** | wagen |
| **(to) deafen:** | taub machen |
| **(to) decipher:** | entziffern |
| **deep in thought:** | gedankenverloren |
| **(to) deny:** | leugnen |
| **determined:** | entschlossen |
| **device:** | Gerät |
| **directions:** | Wegbeschreibung |
| **doggedly:** | verbissen, hartnäckig |
| **do you mind:** | stört es dich (euch) |

| | |
|---|---|
| **(to) drone on**: | eintönig reden |
| **(to) drop out**: | abbrechen |
| **(to) embarrass**: | blamieren |
| **emergency lights**: | Blaulicht |
| **(to) encourage**: | ermutigen |
| **(to) erupt**: | ausbrechen |
| **(to) exclaim**: | ausrufen |
| **(to) exit**: | verlassen |
| **expensive**: | teuer |
| **(to) favor (am.) / favour (brit.)**: | bevorzugen |
| **(to) fill in for sb.**: | für jdn. einspringen |
| **(to) flatter**: | schmeicheln |
| **(to) force**: | aufbrechen |
| **fountain**: | Springbrunnen |
| **fries (am.) / chips (brit).**: | Pommes frites |
| **(to) fumble**: | wühlen, suchen |
| **fumes**: | Dämpfe |
| **(to) furrow**: | runzeln |
| **gadget**: | Gerät |
| **garbage (am.) / rubbish (brit.)**: | Abfall, Müll |
| **(to) get beaten up**: | verprügelt werden |
| **(to) glance**: | einen Blick werfen |
| **gloomy**: | deprimierend |
| **(to) glow**: | strahlen |
| **goon (ugs.)**: | Schläger |
| **(to) grab**: | zufassen |
| **grim**: | finster |
| **grin**: | Grinsen |
| **(to) grumble**: | murren |
| **handsome**: | gut aussehend |
| **hardware store**: | Haushaltswarenladen |
| **he's onto us**: | er ist uns auf die Schliche gekommen |

| | |
|---|---|
| **high-fives (ugs., am.):** | Freudengeste |
| **(to) hiss:** | zischen |
| **(to) hold up in court:** | Beweiskraft vor Gericht haben |
| **Holy Moly:** | Heiliger Bimbam |
| **homework assignment:** | Hausarbeit, Schularbeit |
| **ice cream parlor (am.) / parlour (brit.):** | Eisdiele |
| **ill at ease:** | unbehaglich |
| **impressed:** | beeindruckt |
| **impression:** | Eindruck |
| **incident:** | Vorkommnis |
| **incredible:** | unglaublich |
| **interrogation:** | Vernehmung |
| **(to) investigate:** | ermitteln |
| **invitation:** | Einladung |
| **janitor (am.) / custodian (brit.):** | Hausmeister |
| **(to) kneel:** | knien |
| **lanky:** | schlaksig |
| **(to) launch into:** | in Gang bringen, einleiten |
| **(to) leave his mark:** | Zeichen hinterlassen |
| **locker:** | Schließfach |
| **mansion:** | Villa |
| **maraschino cherry:** | Maraschinokirsche |
| **methamphetamine:** | kristallines Amphetamin |
| **(to) mock:** | verspotten |
| **(to) monitor:** | beaufsichtigen, bewachen |
| **(to) motion:** | winken |
| **muffler (am.) / silencer (brit.):** | Schalldämpfer |
| **(to) mumble:** | murmeln |
| **(to) murmur:** | murmeln |
| **(to) mutter:** | murmeln |
| **(to) nod off (ugs.):** | einnicken |

| | |
|---|---|
| **no kidding (ugs.)**: | im Ernst |
| **(to) occure to sb.**: | jdm. einfallen |
| **(to) offend**: | ärgern |
| **overpowering**: | penetrant |
| **overprotective**: | überbesorgt |
| **page-turner (ugs.)**: | spannendes Buch |
| **passion**: | Inbrunst |
| **(to) pat**: | tätscheln |
| **petite**: | zierlich |
| **(to) pick up**: | aufgreifen |
| **place (ugs.)**: | Haus, Wohnung |
| **pleased**: | zufrieden |
| **porch (am.) / veranda (brit.)** : | Veranda |
| **prized**: | wertvoll |
| **(to) promise**: | versprechen |
| **(to) put my finger on it**: | mit Sicherheit bestimmen |
| **rear**: | hinterer Teil |
| **recovery**: | Gesundung |
| **(to) reek**: | stinken, riechen |
| **(to) relive**: | wieder erleben |
| **restroom (am.) / toilet (brit.)**: | Badezimmer, Toilette |
| **ridge**: | Grat, felsige Erhöhung |
| **rim**: | Rand |
| **rocker**: | Schaukelstuhl |
| **ruefully**: | reumütig |
| **(to) scold**: | tadeln |
| **scoop**: | Kugel |
| **secret**: | Geheimnis |
| **(to) seize**: | greifen |
| **(to) set**: | untergehen |
| **shabby**: | schäbig |
| **sheepishly**: | verlegen |
| **(to) shine**: | scheinen |

| | |
|---|---|
| **shiner (ugs.):** | blaues Auge |
| **(to) show up:** | auftauchen, erscheinen |
| **(to) shrug:** | mit den Achseln zucken |
| **(to) sigh:** | seufzen |
| **skinny:** | dünn |
| **skull and crossbones:** | Totenkopf und gekreuzte Knochen |
| **(to) slap:** | einen Klaps geben |
| **sleuth:** | Detektiv, Spürhund |
| **(to) sling:** | werfen |
| **slope:** | Böschung |
| **(to) smack sb. one (ugs.):** | jdm. eine scheuern |
| **smugly:** | selbstgefällig |
| **(to) snap:** | knacken |
| **(to) snore:** | schnarchen |
| **squad car:** | Streifenwagen |
| **squealing:** | quietschend |
| **stain:** | Fleck |
| **(to) stammer:** | stottern |
| **(to) stare at sb.:** | jdn. anstarren |
| **(to) startle:** | aufschrecken |
| **stealthy:** | verstohlen, heimlich |
| **(to) stomp:** | stapfen |
| **stout:** | korpulent |
| **(to) stow:** | verstauen |
| **(to) strew:** | verstreuen |
| **(to) stroll:** | schlendern |
| **(to) strum:** | klimpern |
| **(to) stumble:** | stolpern |
| **(to) suggest:** | vorschlagen |
| **(to) summon:** | rufen |
| **(to) survey:** | begutachten |
| **suspect:** | Verdächtiger |
| **suspicion:** | Argwohn, Verdacht |
| **(to) swallow:** | schlucken |

| | |
|---|---|
| **(to) tease**: | hänseln |
| **timid**: | schüchtern |
| **(to) tiptoe**: | schleichen |
| **tire (am.) / tyre (brit.)**: | Reifen |
| **tomboy**: | Wildfang |
| **torn**: | zerrissen |
| **(to) toss**: | werfen |
| **(to) trail**: | verfolgen |
| **trailer park (am.) / caravan site (brit.)**: | Wohnwagensiedlung |
| **(to) tremble**: | zittern |
| **trial**: | Gerichtsverfahren |
| **tune**: | Melodie |
| **(to) turn down**: | leise stellen |
| **(to) twist**: | sich winden |
| **two-faced**: | falsch, heuchlerisch |
| **(to) unplug**: | den Stecker herausziehen |
| **unsupervised**: | unbeaufsichtigt |
| **(to) urge**: | drängen |
| **vacant**: | leer stehend |
| **(to) vandalize**: | zerstören |
| **waistband**: | Hosenbund |
| **walk-in closet (am.) / cupboard, wardrobe (brit.)**: | großer Wandschrank |
| **(to) whine**: | winseln |
| **wide-eyed**: | mit großen Augen |
| **wimp (ugs.)**: | Schwächling |
| **winding**: | gewunden |
| **(to) wipe one's brow**: | sich über die Stirn fahren |
| **wiry**: | drahtig |
| **with a twinkle**: | augenzwinkernd |
| **wristwatch**: | Armbanduhr |
| **(to) yawn**: | gähnen |
| **(to) yell**: | schreien, brüllen |
| **(to) zip**: | flitzen |